THE STORY OF MY HEART

By the same author

MOTHERS, FATHERS AND CHILDREN

ḤIKÁYAT-I-DIL

The Hand of the Cause ʻAlí-Akbar Furútan at the Pilgrim House in Haifa, 1982

THE STORY OF MY HEART

Memoirs
of

‘Alí-Akbar Furútan

(ḤIKÁYAT-I-DIL)

translated by
Mahnaz Aflatooni Javid

GEORGE RONALD, Publisher
46 High Street, Kidlington, Oxford, OX5 2DN

ISBN 0-85398-114-0 (Hardcover)
ISBN 0-85398-115-9 (Softcover)

Set by Sunrise Setting in Bembo 11½ on 13 point
Printed in Great Britain

To my dear wife

Ataieh

for her loving assistance

Contents

List of Illustrations

Foreword and Acknowledgements

This book is a translation of *Ḥikáyat-i-Dil*, my memoirs first published in Iran in 1977, but more than a translation for many incidents have been added and the structure of several chapters rearranged.

Personal memoirs cannot be recorded without the use of the word 'I', except by substituting such awkward terms as 'this humble servant' and 'this unworthy person', but my purpose has not been an egotistic one but rather to record memories, talks, and certain events and facts which may possess interest for future generations and encourage youth of today to persevere in and widen the range of their own services to mankind in these years of its danger and trial.

The few extracts from letters by the beloved Guardian, Shoghi Effendi, are included to show that my activities were guided by his instructions rather than my own initiatives.

As much as possible I have omitted the names of the many whom I met and who assisted me, to avoid discrimination, although from ancient times it has been said that 'whoever writes will be the target of arrows'.

Especially in the later pages of the book, which record my work after 1951, I am indebted to various Bahá'í publications such as *The Bahá'í World, Bahá'í International News Service*, the American *Bahá'í News* and official journals of the Alaskan, Australian and Canadian Bahá'ís, from whose columns I have freely borrowed and sometimes quoted reports of my travels and teaching.

I wish also to acknowledge the assistance so willingly

given at the Bahá'í World Centre, particularly by the Research Department in connection with the translation of passages from Bahá'í Writings in Persian and Arabic which are unavailable in English books, and the Audio-Visual Department which sought and reproduced the many photographs. Several other friends, above all the translator, have devoted long hours in preparing the manuscript for publication. To them all I express my sincere gratitude.

All that is left to say is that I have tried my best and now can only beg my readers to look at the intention of these memoirs and not just to words and phrases. The Centre of the Covenant, 'Abdu'l-Bahá, in His Tablet of Visitation has revealed: 'Make me as dust in the pathway of Thy loved ones . . . ' What, then, should we say for ourselves?

'Alí-Akbar Furútan

Haifa, Israel
June 1983

1

My Childhood in Sabzivár

When my father, Karbilá'í Muḥammad-'Alíy-i-Sabzivárí, declared his faith in the Cause of the Blessed Beauty (Bahá'u'lláh), my mother Ṣughrá and my paternal grandmother Maryam, who were both fanatical Shí'ih Muslims, vehemently opposed him to the extent that my grandmother went to the mujtahid of Sabzivár to seek the death sentence of her only son who, in her opinion, had become a heretic and a heathen. The efforts of the well-known Bahá'í teachers of the time such as Mr Furúghí and others proved to be of no avail and failed to bring any change in their attitude.

One day in Sabzivár one of the non-Muslim merchants who was accused of having an immoral relationship with a Muslim woman was killed in public in a most atrocious way. At the same time, while the city was still in a state of excitement and people were enraged, the mob captured my father and ruthlessly dragged him to the house of the mujtahid to seek the death sentence for him so that they could burn the body of the Bábí* with the corpse of the non-Muslim merchant, and in this way secure the reward of heaven for themselves. The mujtahid who was a simple-hearted and good-natured man refused to issue the death sentence on the grounds that my father might be mentally unbalanced, and succeeded in dispersing the crowd with his exhortations and admonitions.

My father, after escaping from the claws of the ignorant, went home only to face the abusive language of his mother:

* At that time the Bahá'ís were still called Bábís by most people.

why was he not dead to free their family honour from disgrace and shame?

This miserable family situation continued for many years until one night my mother had a dream in which an Imam with a radiant countenance and piercing eyes appeared to her. My mother hastily ran to him to pay her respects but the Imam declared that she should leave him as 'thou art not one of our faithful Shí'ihs'. My mother then clung to his garment and tearfully said, 'May my life be a sacrifice to thee, I have not neglected my religious duties. I have continually attended the commemoration of the martyrs of Karbilá. I have always been present at those gatherings mourning the martyrdom of the Prince of Martyrs (Imam Ḥusayn). My children and I are always busy visiting the shrines of the Holy Ones. I have continually given offerings. What wrong have my hands wrought that thou dost not permit me to be in thy presence?' The Imam replied, 'All thou hast mentioned is true; however, for what reason hast thou afflicted thy husband who hast believed in the Promised One [the Qá'im], who treadeth the Straight Path? And why hast thou tormented him with a new torment every moment?' My mother then wept in her sleep and the Imam disappeared.

The cries of my mother awoke my grandmother, and in response to her question as to the cause of this weeping and wailing, my mother recounted her dream. It was the hour of dawn and they both went to my father's room and related to him what had passed. From her description my father understood that the Imam in my mother's dream was no One but 'Abdu'l-Bahá and asked my mother whether she could recognize the Imam if she saw His picture. He then unveiled to her the portrait of the Master which lay hidden with the Bahá'í books in a safe cupboard. My mother confirmed whole-heartedly that the Imam was indeed the same Person. My father then, for the hundredth time, began to recount the Master's life and the beliefs of the people of Bahá. Fortunately, at that hour of dawn, they finally awoke from their slumber and the light of faith illumined their hearts and souls.

After this event, my mother and grandmother arose to compensate for what they had done, and our house became a refuge for those Bahá'ís who, like my father in the past, lacked peace and security in their own homes. I was five years old then.

When my mother and grandmother declared their belief in the Cause, they conscientiously began to think in terms of the education of their children and promptly sent me and my brother, who was then nine, to the 'school'. I vividly remember that the school of 'Ammih Khánum (literally, Dame Aunt) consisted of a room plastered with straw and mud with only a peep-hole as a window through which a feeble light shone. About fifteen girls and boys sat on whatever they themselves had brought from their homes: one on a straw mat, the other on a prayer rug, the third on something else but all with their particular books open in front of them. There were also in the room the wooden instruments for bastinado and pilliwinks* for disciplining the boys and girls when required. In that school I learned to read and write, but after one year I was sent to the school of Mullá Najaf which was only for boys and had stricter discipline and a much heavier programme of study. More than thirty students from six to fifteen years of age attended.

Mullá Najaf was both principal and teacher. He was also busy with various religious duties for the villagers who sought his help, including preaching, consulting the Qur'án for good omens, and copying prayers for protection. Since we were in school from early morning till dusk, we brought

* A method used in schools to punish girls, the bastinado being used for boys.

our own lunches. I remember that after lunch Mullá Najaf would wrap his cloak around him, lie down, and order us to memorize our lessons while he took a nap. Sometimes this nap lasted until sunset when we would sing a rhyme we had composed: 'Ho, Ho, it is time to go!' until he raised his head from under his cloak and issued the decree of our freedom.

We had a tradition in Sabzivár that students could go to homes where a new baby was born, sing a welcoming song for the child, receive in return candy and money, and then offer their earnings to their teacher in exchange for a free day from school. So we were always actively alert, and as soon as we learned of a new-born child, we rushed there, sang the famous song – 'May the peace of God rest on your moon-like face; may the Commander of the Faithful [Imam 'Alí] be your protector' – received our gifts and ran to our teacher to buy one free day. Of course, such a bounty was not always easy to come by. Sometimes the students of two or three other schools would find out about the same house. Then war was declared on the streets as each tried to reach the house before the others, because it was also a part of the tradition that only one group could enter and sing, and everybody was well aware of this restriction.

After one year I was transferred from this school to a *Mu'allim-Khánih* (House of Teachers). It was a newly-built school in western style and had a principal, a supervisor, benches, blackboard, a break between subjects, and so forth. The name of our *Mu'allim-Khánih* was 'Alavíyyih, and its curriculum included arithmetic, history, geography and chemistry, in addition to customary studies. We even had a teacher who taught French and we called him 'Monsieur'! I remember one afternoon when all the students had lined up for the last review of the day by the new supervisor who had just come from Tehran. I was happy and jolly and quite busy talking and laughing with a student beside me. I think we were making faces at each other when the supervisor, by an unfortunate chance, caught us, and assuming that I was mocking him ordered the custodian of the school to bring the bastinado. My feet were whipped so many times that they were covered with blood and I had to be carried home on the back of a porter. After this incident I did not return to the *Mu'allim-Khánih* and later heard that the supervisor was discharged from his duties in Sabzivár and transferred back to Tehran.

During this interval at home I heard from a friend who was visiting me that a 'fiery carriage' which moved without horses was brought to Sabzivár. I was greatly astonished and, with the permission of my mother, my friend and I went to the bazaar to see it. At the centre of the covered bazaar there was an inn in which the 'fiery carriage' was housed. They had placed circles of ropes around it so that nobody could go close to it. Also, at the entrance to the inn there stood a man in a khaki cloak and brown head-dress, with a whip in his hand. Being curious, I passed through the crowd of spectators, went under the rope, and entered the forbidden zone. No sooner had I done this than I felt a painful burning on my back. I turned my head to see what had happened; the man with the whip was about to strike a second blow over my almost bare back. Like a flash of lightning I left that dangerous place, but for many hours continued to remember the impressive sight of the 'fiery carriage' and the burning sensation on my back.

Sabzivár, like Yazd, was known then as 'the City of Worship' and 'the City of Believers', and its residents showed the utmost fanaticism in carrying out their visible religious duties. For this reason my father, who was then known as Muḥammad-'Alíy-i-Bábí, was continually harassed by the people, and peace and quiet were altogether absent from our house. I clearly remember that our house was located in an area where many idle children wandered about all the time. On summer nights when we slept on our roof, they would gather around our house and sing with a colloquial accent and deafening voices, 'We want no Bábí around, we want no Bábí around.' Then after their insane shoutings they would set a number of cotton balls moistened with kerosene on fire and throw them at our beds. We often had to flee from the roof on those hot summer nights and seek refuge in the stuffy rooms.

It was during one of these summer nights while we were having our dinner that we heard a most vigorous knock at our door. My father went down and we left our dinner and came out on the terrace to see what was happening. A short man in a government uniform and a tall skin hat greeted my father by slapping him on his face, and with a stream of insulting words said, 'Now your puppy dogs (children) have become so daring that they beat my children. Don't you know that I work for the government and can do whatever I please with you?' My father, who was a tall, strong man with broad shoulders, mildly told him, 'Shame on you Karbilá'í Ḥusayn. We are neighbours. My children have not even set eyes on the streets these days. These are absolutely false accusations.' But Karbilá'í Ḥusayn would not stop his shouting, continuing 'Now you call me a liar, you irreligious Bábí?' By this time all the neighbours had come to watch the show, and my father with the same resignation and meekness said, 'Look, I am twice as tall and ten times as strong as you. I can finish you with only one slap, but I will not because my Beloved has forbidden me to do so. So just go home.' Finally, the short man, still yelling and screaming, left and my father rejoined us. We did not finish our dinner and, half hungry, with the dreadful face of the short man dancing in front of our eyes, we went to bed.

That, however, was not the end of the story. A few days later, one of my father's Muslim friends came to inform him that two people were determined to set our house on fire. He advised us to shut the door to our garden securely and take every precaution. But after he left, my father firmly insisted that on the contrary the door to our house would always be left open to welcome our unexpected guests! And although nothing happened, my brother and I did not sleep at all and fearfully hid ourselves in the protective bosoms of our mother and grandmother all night long.

2

Twelve Years in 'Ishqábád

One night my grandmother had a dream of the Master in which he guided our family to leave Iran and pioneer to 'Ishqábád (Ashkabad). Immediately after that dream we began to prepare for the journey. My father closed his business and, after receiving permission from Mashhad to cross the border, we set out on our adventure. My entire family, which consisted of my father Muḥammad-'Alí, my mother Ṣughrá, my grandmother Maryam, my oldest brother Muḥammad-Ḥusayn, my younger brothers 'Alí-Aṣghar and 'Abbás-'Alí, and myself left Sabzivár early in April 1914. Mounted on a wagon which was usually used to transfer dried fruits and cotton, we reached 'Ishqábád on the ninth day of Riḍván.

On the very day of our arrival, my oldest brother and I accompanied my father and another believer to the Mashriqu'l-Adhkár to participate in the celebration of the Feast of Riḍván. The school for boys, which was located in the vicinity of that blessed Temple, was adorned with all kinds of flowers and carpeted with the most exquisite rugs. The garden of the Mashriqu'l-Adhkár truly resembled paradise. Coming from the oppressive environment of Sabzivár to such a haven, we were thoroughly astonished and dumbfounded and did not know what to do with ourselves. Needless to say, after hearing the chanting of the prayers, listening to the speakers who talked on this occasion, and also after enjoying the abundant refreshments, we returned to our new home with a joy we had never experienced before.

The Bahá'ís of 'I<u>sh</u>qábád owned two schools at that time, one for girls and another for boys, and both of these were located in the vicinity of the Temple. I was nine years old then, and although I could read and write in Persian, because I did not know any Russian I was placed in the first grade. My education began in 1914 and ended four years later, when I was asked to teach the first-graders. I continued this service through 1922, but in the following year I began my secondary education and graduated late in 1925.

It is appropriate at this point to include an excerpt from a Tablet of 'Abdu'l-Bahá concerning the schools at 'I<u>sh</u>qábád:

O ye of high resolve and noble aims! Your letter was eloquent, its contents original and sensitively expressed, and it betokened your great and praiseworthy efforts to educate the children, both girls and boys. This is among the most important of all human endeavours. Every possible means of education must be made available to Bahá'í children, tender plants of the Divine garden, for in this consisteth the illumination of humankind.

Praised be God, the friends in 'I<u>sh</u>qábád have laid a solid foundation, an unassailable base. It was in the City of Love* that the first Bahá'í House of Worship was erected; and today in this city the means for the education of children are also being developed . . . Now must ye widen the scope of your endeavours and draw up plans to establish schools for higher education, so that the City of Love will become the Bahá'í focal centre for science and arts . . .

Devote ye particular attention to the school for girls, for the greatness of this wondrous Age will be manifested as a result of progress in the world of women . . .

Instruction in the schools must begin with instruction in religion. Following religious training, and the binding of the child's heart to the love of God, proceed with his education in the other branches of knowledge. (*Compilation on Bahá'í Education*, p. 37.)

* Literal translation of 'I<u>sh</u>qábád. 'The name of the city', 'Abdu'l-Bahá is reported as saying, 'is a beautiful one. 'I<u>sh</u>qábád's situation is significant in the geography of Asia. Marv and 'I<u>sh</u>qábád are in fact the most important cities in that area.' (*Raḥíq-i-Ma<u>kh</u>túm*, vol. 2, pp. 312–13.)

Also, the Local Spiritual Assembly of 'Ishqábád in its circular letter of 1897 recorded an account of the Bahá'í schools of that city. The following excerpts are from this letter:

The Government authorities, among other schools, extended their invitation to the Bahá'í school [for boys], which has now been in operation for three years, to participate in a country-wide celebration observed in honour of one of the well-known poets of Russia. Before the inauguration of the celebration, the Bahá'í students were called to a gathering held in the garden of the Military Club. When the Governor of the Upper Caspian Sea Region came to the garden, all the students were called to meet him. The Governor, who was a respected man, kindly asked each student his name and the duration of his education in the school, and later, upon his instruction, a group picture of the students was taken the next day in the same garden and sent to St Petersburg.

On the concluding night of the celebration when the public, soldiers, officers, and Government dignitaries had gathered in the large square of the city, the Bahá'í students entered the square in official uniforms and recited an anthem that had been composed for that particular occasion. The recitation was so well-received that upon the request of the people it was repeated at the end of the programme. When the fireworks began, the Bahá'í students were placed in the first row so that they could see them without difficulty.

A few days after the conclusion of this celebration, the Commander-in-Chief of Turkistan arrived in 'Ishqábád. On that day, representatives of the various communities went to meet and welcome him at the train station, and a group of Bahá'ís also decided to greet him. The Governor of the Upper Caspian Sea Region introduced the Bahá'ís, and the Commander-in-Chief kindly asked a few questions about the Bahá'í schools and stated that he had heard complimentary remarks about them and had seen the picture of the students.

On the third day of his visit, the Municipal Office notified us that the Commander-in-Chief would visit the school. At one hour before noon, in the company of the Governor of 'Ishqábád and other dignitaries, the Commander-in-Chief came to the school. Two of the students read the school report in Russian and Persian. Then the Commander posed a mathematical problem to one of the students which the student accurately solved on the blackboard. The Commander presented him with a gold medal, and expressed his satisfaction and appreciation of the school administrators . . . The news reporters present on that day published the events of this visit in great detail, and the fame of the Cause of God was spread even further.

For the information of my readers, a brief history of 'Ishqábád follows. In the middle of the sixth century BC the army of Cyrus the Great passed through (what is part of Russia today) and conquered the area presently known as 'Ishqábád. After the passing of two centuries Alexander the Great conquered Persia and added this territory to the rest of his empire. One hundred and fifty years later the Parthians took over the region and built the famous city of Nísá with its magnificent palaces and majestic buildings, eighteen kilometres outside 'Ishqábád. Ibn-i-Ḥawqal described it, in *Ṣuratu'l-Arḍ*, as 'a large city, very prosperous, green and pleasant'. (It has also been known as Nísiyih or Nísí.) This region changed hands many times in the next few hundred years until in the second half of the seventh century AD the Arabs conquered the entire area of Central Asia. In the ninth century AD, the Samanids captured this region and were followed by Seljuks in the eleventh century who conquered the entire Persian Empire, Caucasus, Iraq, Syria, the peninsula of Asia Minor and all of Central Asia, which included the 'Ishqábád of today.

The extensive empire of the Seljuks began to deteriorate at the beginning of the twelfth century when the Middle East was invaded by the bloodthirsty Genghiz Khan and later by Tamerlane towards the end of the fourteenth century. Their empire disintegrated further after the passing of a century, and local governments such as Bukhara and

Khiva, and stronger countries like Iran regained their independence, and for a while 'Ishqábád changed hands between these local and national governments. In the second half of the nineteenth century, the Russian Empire began to expand its territory in Central Asia, and the Tsar's army conquered extensive territories in Sar-Dar'ya, Zeravshan and Amu-Dar'ya. In 1869 the 'Ishqábád region was also annexed to these territories, and when in 1881 the Russian army captured the citadel of Gúg-Tappih and the district of 'Ishqábád, its victory was complete. Three years later the inhabitants of that city accepted Russian citizenship. In 1881 Turkmenistan of today was named the Upper Caspian Sea Region (Transcaspia) and 'Ishqábád was chosen as its seat. In 1898 it was annexed to Turkistan which includes all of Central Asia.

In 1881 the population of 'Ishqábád consisted of 500 families; in 1884, 4,000 families; in 1886, excluding military personnel, 10,000; in 1897, 20,000; in 1926, 52,000; in 1939, 127,000; in 1959, 169,000; and in 1968, 244,000 families.

I have many recollections of my stay in 'Ishqábád, of which I will recount only a few:

1. I recall that during one of the very hot summers I decided for the first time to take a trip outside of 'Ishqábád, and with the permission of my parents I took the train and went to Gúg-Tappih where a group of Bahá'ís had businesses. I was fifteen years old at the time, and one of the Bahá'ís who was a friend of my family entertained me graciously. I spent the days with him at his place of business and slept on the roof of his shop at nights. During one of the very hot days when the heat of the sun was roasting everyone, a Turkman wearing his tribal costume of cloak, sash, fur hat and long boots came to my host's shop. After exchanging the customary pleasantries, he told my host that his young daughter was ill in Obá, where the tribe had

pitched its tents, and unable to reach a physician he had come to beg my host, who had experience of herbal remedies, to pay her a visit and free his family of their torment. My host tried very hard to excuse himself, but failing he finally consented, and under the burning heat of the midday sun we mounted our two donkeys and with the Turkman on his horse we began our journey. We passed the sandy and dry desert to reach his settlement and, after having spent a few moments of rest by the stream which passed through his garden, we visited the patient.

She was a young girl who was lying in the middle of the tent with her tearful mother at her side. My host suggested to the Turkman in his dialect that they engage in prayer and beg God for healing instead of trying to prescribe a medicine, and added that the Bahá'ís had a prayer which they could recite on such occasions to beseech God, the Almighty, for His balm and healing. After this explanation, my host signalled to me, and I began to recite a healing prayer in a clear and loud voice. Whenever I spoke the word 'healing', the girl who could apparently understand its meaning would sigh, open her eyes and look upward submissively as if expecting something. From all her movements it was evident that she was trusting wholly in the Lord of all the world and the Creator of the heavens and earth. When the prayer was said we retired from the tent and, after eating some grapes that the Turkman had brought us as token of his appreciation, left the settlement. A few days later, the Turkman came happily to give us the glad-tidings of the recovery of his daughter.

2. I was fifteen years old when I was appointed to the National Youth Committee and elected its secretary. But I was so inexperienced that on one occasion I remember having rewritten one of the Committee letters more than ten times, and even then, when I showed the letter to our chairman for approval, he instructed me to rewrite it again!

I gradually learned my lesson in writing letters, but never succeeded in demonstrating much improvement in my calligraphy! This same Committee founded a news-sheet called *Fikr-i-Javán*. I wrote many articles for it and submitted humorous stories under fictitious names. These articles and stories were well received by youth and adults, and gradually prepared me for my future contribution to *Khurshíd-i-Khávar* (Sun of the Orient) magazine.

3. One night in a youth meeting a non-Bahá'í Persian, who had finished his higher education in Germany and was on his way to Tehran, unexpectedly joined us. After hearing the talk of one of the youth, which was less than eloquent and was presented in a mixture of Persian and foreign words, he stood up and without permission of the chairman began to condemn strongly our ignorance of the 'sweet Persian tongue'. At the suggestion of Áqá Siyyid Mihdíy-i-Gulpáygání who was present in the meeting, I left my seat and began to answer his criticism, using the eloquent language of the sacred Writings and also the literary compositions of Mírzá Abu'l-Faḍl. When I had finished my talk, our Persian guest arose and facing the radiant eyes of those present, particularly the youth, began to praise my knowledge of Persian, and offered his apologies for what he had said.

4. The Local Spiritual Assembly of Bádkúbih (Baku) had requested the Local Spiritual Assembly of 'Ishqábád to send them a Bahá'í, a young man familiar with Turkish and Russian and versed in modern sciences, to teach the Faith in that city. Mr Gulpáygání most kindly selected me for this assignment and I began my journey by taking the train to Krasnovodsk* and then by ship to Bádkúbih. After reaching the city, I took a carriage to the Ḥaẓíratu'l-Quds, which at the time was called Musáfir-Khánih (Guest House)

* Kazil-Su, a port on the Caspian Sea, was conquered by the Russians in 1865. The name means 'Red Water', as does the present Russian name.

and asked the custodian, a man of the Lesghi tribe named Áqá Taqí, to direct me to the chairman of the Local Assembly. He told me that at 4.00 p.m. every day he would come to his office in the same building, and I waited there for him. At exactly four a tall, slender and handsome man arrived. After ascertaining that he was the chairman of the Assembly, I approached him and gave him my letter of introduction. He asked me where the Bahá'í teacher was as he could not imagine that the teacher sent was indeed this nineteen-year-old youth in his school uniform standing in front of him. Bashfully, I answered that I was the Bahá'í teacher. (Our conversation was held in Turkish.) After an exchange of pleasantries, he ordered Áqá Taqí to guide me to a room in the upper floor of the building designated for teachers of the Cause. He took me to a large hall adorned with a portrait of the Master, and immediately after putting my suitcase down, began to dance excitedly in front of the portrait, saying, 'May my life be a sacrifice to Thee, O 'Abdu'l-Bahá. After this, the babes of the cradle will arise to teach the Cause!'

I stayed in Bádkúbih for three months and the teaching activities proved to be very successful. Every day from sunrise to sunset, and at times till midnight, talks were held with seekers, and during this time thirteen educated youth declared their faith in the Cause, and many others became informed and interested. This is the secret of 'Abdu'l-Bahá's utterance that if one arises to teach, no matter how inexperienced he may be, he will be confirmed and successful.

5. In 1925 I was about to set out for Moscow to enter its university for my higher education when I was invited to meet with the Spiritual Assembly. The Assembly had appointed me principal of the Bahá'í schools and kindergartens, but since the Spiritual Assembly of Bádkúbih had again invited me to go to that city to continue the teaching

work, the ‘Ishqábád Assembly consulted and decided to leave the final decision to me. After praying and talking with my father, I preferred to engage in the teaching activities instead of accepting the school appointment, but on the day that I went to meet with the Assembly to notify them of my decision something happened that changed the course of events. On my way, I passed by my father's workshop as usual but to my astonishment I found it closed. I questioned a neighbour and learned that he had been taken to prison because of a delay in the payment of his taxes. I hurried to the police station and found my old father with his snow-white beard and innocent face behind iron bars. I was deeply grieved and, telling myself that I could not possibly leave my old and feeble father to the care of others, I made up my mind to stay in ‘Ishqábád and promote the goals of the schools and support my family at the same time. I told my father that I had to meet the Assembly, but after that I would instantly come to free him from prison. I went to the meeting and announced my decision, which made everyone extremely happy, and I was offered many prayers and much praise.

On leaving the Assembly, I immediately started for the police station, but to my amazement when I passed my father's workshop on my way, I found it open with my father busy at work. This looked to me almost like a magician's trick and I asked my father what had happened. He replied that as soon as I had gone he was set free, with apologies for having arrested him for someone else. In short, this incident, as became evident later, completely changed the course of my spiritual and worldly life.

Consequently I stayed in ‘Ishqábád and became principal of the two schools for boys and girls and the two Bahá'í kindergartens, and continued this service for a year. During this year, 1925, a group of expert speakers came from the capital to ‘Ishqábád to promote materialism and challenge religious ideologies. Every night they held meetings in the large assembly hall of the city and talked to the audience which represented various religions and creeds. The Local Spiritual Assembly wisely recommended that Bahá'ís listen attentively to the speakers but refrain from participating in the discussions and arguments of the audience. One night, however, one of the speakers addressed the Bahá'ís in the course of his talk, saying that evidently there were a great number of Bahá'ís in 'Ishqábád who had built a most exquisite Temple, and whose educational facilities were well known and much respected, and he asked why the Bahá'ís were not present in the meetings to discuss their beliefs. He then formally extended his invitation to the Bahá'í community to take part in the debates. The insistence of the speakers and the requests of other religious communities, such as Christian and Muslim, impelled the Assembly to review its decision, and Jináb-i-Siyyid Mihdíy-i-Gulpáygání was appointed to represent the Bahá'í community. Following the example of the Master, using logical reasoning and proofs, Mr Gulpáygání succeeded in demonstrating the existence of God and the truth of His Messengers. His lectures were so effective that no one uttered a word of argument, and those who agreed were most thankful. Thus the fame of the Cause spread even more as a result.

6. When the devastating news of the passing of the Master reached 'Ishqábád the Assembly announced a week of mourning, and the news was announced to the public through daily newspapers both in Turkish and Russian.

The Assembly Hall to the north of the House of Worship was prepared to receive guests, and the portrait of the Master and the pillars of the Assembly Hall were covered with black cloth. The members of the organizing committee all wore black armbands and quietly received and guided the guests. Every day a great number of Bahá'ís and a number of non-Bahá'ís came to the meetings. Prayers were melodiously chanted, and speakers tried to console the grief-stricken friends. At times one could hear the sad cries of those who had lost their Master. One day during this week of mourning, the students of Muẓẓaffarí School, which belonged to non-Bahá'í Persians and was administered and supervised by the Consulate of Iran, together with their teachers and principal, all wearing black armbands, came to convey their condolences. Also, the mujtahid of the Iranian Shí'ihs, the religious leader of the Caucasus Muslims, and another Muslim preacher who had not visited the Mashriqu'l-Adhkár before, came to express their sympathy on that occasion.

7. The Bahá'í children and youth of 'Ishqábád were in great need of a capable teacher to foster their spiritual growth and, by deepening them in the sacred Writings, protect their young minds and hearts from doubt and misunderstanding. One of the blessed individuals who contributed extensively to their need was Mr Gulpáygání. This respected scholar was a nephew of Mírzá Abu'l-Faḍl, and for years was editor of *Khurshíd-i-Khávar* and chairman of the Local Spiritual Assembly of 'Ishqábád. He was an able writer, a superior speaker, a gifted poet, and a prudent thinker respected by friends and strangers alike. Like many other youth of that time, I was also a fisherman in the ocean of his immense knowledge, and attended the classes and discussion meetings of that kind and beloved educator. His instructions and advice so opened my eyes and ears that I was set free from any tendency towards materialistic ideologies, and instead the flame of yearning to immerse myself in the Writings became the companion of every moment of my life. With his encouragement, I spoke in many Bahá'í gatherings and wrote many articles for the Bahá'í magazine.

I would like to take the opportunity at this time, as a

matter of loyalty, to acknowledge my other teachers and to express my appreciation and gratitude to Áqá Shaykh Muḥammad-'Alí, Áqá Shaykh Ḥaydar and Mírzá Taqí Khán-i-Adíb.

8. The Youth Committee had founded a Bahá'í library with reading rooms, known as 'Maḥmúdíyyih', in the vicinity of the Temple. This library was built in memory of Ḥájí Mírzá Maḥmúd-i-Afnán, the son of Ḥájí Mírzá Muḥammad Taqíy-i-Afnán, known as Vakílu'l-Ḥaqq and Vakílu'd-Dawlih, the founder of the Mashriqu'l-Adhkár of 'Ishqábád, the first Bahá'í House of Worship in the world. It was open to Bahá'ís and non-Bahá'ís alike, and I was the custodian and manager of that important undertaking.

9. In 1922 a group of well-known Russian actors came to 'Ishqábád to perform in the famous Gigant Theatre of that city. The director of this group, also a famous actor, was a certain Orlov whose wife was also an established actress. On the suggestion of a number of Bahá'ís, this group decided to stage Isabel Grinevskaya's poetic drama *The Báb*, and with financial assistance from some of the Bahá'ís and many rehearsals, the play was prepared. On the night of the performance a large audience of Bahá'ís and non-Bahá'ís gathered in the theatre, but at the climax of the play when interest was at its highest, the theatre was suddenly enveloped in darkness. Fortunately, the interruption did not last long and after a few minutes the electricity was restored. It was later found that a few unsympathetic individuals had cut the main power cables on the street to express their hostility in this way. The play, however, continued and was most favourably received.

The author of this drama was a lady from Petrograd who was an extremely talented poetess and dramatist. When she became familiar with the tenets of the Faith, she wrote two plays, namely, *The Báb* and *Bahá'u'lláh*. Both were published and became well known. *The Báb*, which was published in 1903, was first presented in one of the leading theatres of St Petersburg (later, Petrograd) and enthusiastically received by the literary circle of the time. Leo Tolstoy became acquainted with the Cause of God through this play and the favourable articles written about it in the capital, and through correspondence with Mme Grinevskaya he obtained introductory information on the Bahá'í Faith. (See *The Bahá'í World*, vol. IX, pp. 569–70.)

In 1911 Mme Grinevskaya had the honour of meeting 'Abdu'l-Bahá in Alexandria, and was His guest for two weeks. On her return she published a book entitled *A Journey in the Countries of the Sun*, which included the account of her meeting with the Master.

The Báb was again staged in The People's Theatre of Petrograd in 1917. A great number of persons came from Turkistan and Moscow to see it, among them ambassadors of foreign countries including China, and many of them carried the second edition of the drama. Martha Root has written and left to posterity a detailed article on the life and services of Mme Grinevskaya, which was published in *The Bahá'í World*, vol. VI.

3

University Days and Bahá'í Service in Moscow

In the summer of 1926 I went to Moscow to continue my education. I spent one week on the train and, after passing through Turkmenistan, Uzbekistan, Kazakhstan, Kirgizia, Tataristan, and parts of Russian Europe, I arrived in the city of 'one thousand and six hundred churches', with its seven hundred years of history. During that year many students from all over the country had come to the capital to compete in the entrance examination of the university, as the number of applicants by far exceeded the available space, so much so that only one out of fifty applicants could be admitted. However, with the grace and bounty of God, and daily dawn prayers, I passed the examination with honour and began my studies in Education. In addition, through ceaseless confirmations of the Lord of the world, I was also offered an adequate monthly scholarship and a room in student housing facilities, and with all these concerns lifted from my mind, I began to study diligently. At last my long-awaited dream was fulfilled, and I was quite unable to thank God sufficiently for His unfailing assistance.

But my peace of mind only lasted a short while. A few months later I received a letter from the Teaching Committee of 'Ishqábád which greatly disturbed me. In its letter the Committee stated that I was sufficiently qualified to teach the Cause of God, as my previous successful experiences had proved, that I knew Turkish and Russian, and that it was a pity I should spend my precious time acquiring a formal education with uncertain ultimate benefits while in the meantime depriving myself of service to the Cause. After reading this letter I found myself faced with a decision I could not make alone, and therefore I turned to the Spiritual Assembly of Moscow for consultation. The Assembly, on the grounds that this decision could change the course of my life, excused itself from a final recommendation, and suggested that I write to the beloved Guardian and ask for his advice. I obeyed the suggestion of the Assembly and wrote my letter to the Guardian, to which I received the following response:

16 November 1926
The letter of that beloved friend was read by the Guardian of the Cause of God . . . and brought joy to his heart. He spoke of you and praised God that you . . . are assisted by divine confirmations in your education, that you intend to complete it and wish to diffuse the heavenly fragrances, to serve the Faith, and to teach the Cause of God. This intention attracts the confirmations of the One true God and favours of the kingdom of eternity. Therefore, he cherishes the hope that you will eventually attain the goal of your desire . . .

Teaching the Cause of God is possible under all circumstances, even through trade and commerce and through right conduct, as it is said that goodly deeds and a praiseworthy character are in themselves the teachers of the Cause. Therefore, any individual, in whatever profession he may be engaged, if he conducts himself in a praiseworthy manner and exemplifies human perfections, will himself become the sign of the propagation of the Word of God and will hoist the banner of the glory of the Cause.

Concerning the determination of your duty, the Guardian stated that you should in no way be disturbed and distressed, and if in all circumstances you resort and cling to the cord of consultation, you will be confirmed in all your efforts. In any case, you should refer to the Spiritual Assembly and act according to the wishes and approval of its respected and elected members. Whatever the result of the consultation of the Spiritual Assembly may be, that is the correct course of action and the path of the good-pleasure of the Lord of lords, because the Spiritual Assemblies are inspired, assisted, and confirmed, and are institutions expressly ordained in the Text. Therefore, without fear carry out whatever they deem wise, so that you will be confirmed in all your affairs. The beloved Guardian also remembered your parents and prayed for them. This letter was written according to the instructions of the beloved Guardian.

The beloved Guardian wrote the following in his own handwriting on the margin of this letter:

O spiritual Friend:

This servant in this illumined spot prays at the sacred Threshold from the depths of his heart for your peace of mind, prosperity and success, so that you may excel in divine knowledge and material learning . . .

The servant of His Threshold,
Shoghi

Upon receiving the advice of the Guardian, I went back to consult with the Spiritual Assembly. After careful consideration, they decided unanimously that I should continue my education, and thus freed me from my hesitation and doubt. A copy of the letter of the beloved Guardian was sent to the 'Ishqábád Teaching Committee, and they were informed of the decision of the Spiritual Assembly of Moscow.

I should mention at this point that the original of this letter was entrusted to my mother so that it could be sent back safely to Iran. When my mother and brothers returned to Iran, the letter was in turn entrusted to a Bahá'í woman in 'Ishqábád. We later heard that she had passed away, but the fate of the letter of the Guardian remained a mystery. In 1974, however, when I was sent by the Universal House of Justice on a mission to Iran, I met there one of the Bahá'ís of 'Ishqábád who had come to visit his relatives. In the course of our conversation I mentioned the letter of the beloved Guardian and expressed my grief at its loss. He informed me that he had the original and promised to send it to me on his return to ‘Ishqábád. He also gave me an account of the fate of this precious treasure during the intervening years. This noble gentleman honoured his promise and I received this invaluable letter in two months.

Now I would like to mention a dozen memories of my time in Moscow, including various journeys:

1. On the way to Moscow by train we encountered such a severe snowstorm in Kazakhstan that the railway lines were closed and the train shook to the galloping winds. One of our companions was a Bahá'í mother with a nursing baby. We had no access to food and water in that storm, and when all the food, and naturally the milk, was consumed, the baby came close to death. On the suggestion of another friend, he and I decided to leave the train and try to find a station attendant in an attempt to get some milk. In that incredible storm, we put on whatever warm clothes we had, wrapped a blanket around our heads and, taking a metal kettle with us, left the train wholly trusting in God. The wind was so icy and strong that we were thrown from side to side and my gloved hand holding the kettle hurt me badly. We finally saw the smoke of a chimney in the distance, and after much effort reached the house. It was indeed the house of one of the station attendants who, with his wife and three children, was astonished to see us. We told our story and asked for their help. His wife, herself a mother, nobly and smilingly shared some of her children's food and poured into our kettle some milk, which under these conditions was as rare as gold. I cannot convey the happiness of our Bahá'í mother when we gave her the milk. The storm continued for another two days after which the lines were cleared and we continued our journey.

2. In the winter of 1927, when I returned to ‘Ishqábád to spend my winter recess with my parents, I found my father

severely ill in bed. I was told that all the doctors had lost hope and there was nothing else they could do. Hearing this I rushed to his bedside and sat quietly by him, but after looking at his radiant face, I lost my control and tears rolled from my eyes. My father gave a deep sigh, opened his tired eyes and addressed me: 'My son, I may never see you again. Therefore, I want to express my last wishes to you and ask you to listen carefully and try your best to carry them out.' He then continued, 'I wish to dedicate one of my sons to the Cause so that after me, detached from all material concerns, he will spend his life in service to the Faith. I have chosen you, my second son, for this purpose, and my wish for you is that after you have completed your education you will engage in nothing else but Bahá'í activities. You must give me a Bahá'í promise at this moment, and pledge that you will carry out my wishes.' With tears in my eyes I told my beloved father his wish was indeed my true desire and I would obey him then and for ever. He became very happy when he heard this, prayed for me and, taking his Bahá'í ring with the Greatest Name from his finger, gave it to me as the sign of the covenant between us.

Not too long after my visit I received the news of his passing. A befitting memorial service was held in his memory which all the friends of Moscow attended. He is buried in the Bahá'í cemetery of 'Is͟hqábád.

3. I was the only Persian, and the only Bahá'í, in the Faculty of Education, and used to hold discussions with my professors whenever I heard them mention anything contrary to my beliefs. One day my Psychology professor gave a lecture on dreams and, while refuting the immortality of the soul, suggested that the source of dreams could be traced to our daily activities and environmental influences. After the class was over I approached him and with his permission stated that I did not agree with what he had said, as history has recorded many instances where certain indi-

viduals have had visions of future events. I argued that many of these visions, left to posterity in explicit or in allegorical language, have fully materialized, sometimes thousands of years later, and mentioned as proof the revelations of St John and the prophecies of Daniel and the Imams of Islam, recorded in their books, as examples of such true visions in which the Prophets seemed to witness the very events they foretold. I then asked how, if we consider the dream to be only the repetition of daily activities and limit its source to material causes, we can explain these extraordinary phenomena? My elderly professor paused for a long time and finally said that psychology has as yet no answer to such questions and perhaps future research will shed light on them and other unsolved problems. Then with a meaningful smile he added that I had made him doubt his own stand on this issue and, warmly shaking my hand, he departed.

4. Pushkin, the famous poet of Russia, composed a well-known and beautiful ballad, 'Imitations of the Qur'án', based on verses of this Holy Book. At the same time he discreetly criticized the Prophet of Islam as a gifted poet but bereft of a knowledge of astronomy, pointing to those verses of the Qur'án that refer to the darkening of the moon and the uniting of the sun and moon. (See Rodwell, Sura LXXV:8–9.) I once gave a talk to a large number of students, attended also by my Literature professor, defending the Prophet Muḥammad. I said that Pushkin was perhaps ignorant of the intricacies of the Qur'án and the spiritual allusions made in that Book, and gave a comprehensive review of terms used by mystics and Sufis. This talk was favourably received by most of the audience, but a group of students, who considered Pushkin to be the sun of the heaven of literature, did not show much enthusiasm and instead accused me of being superstitious and a religious fanatic.

5. One of my professors of a previous generation, who taught the 'History of Civilization', was relatively apart from materialism and closer to believing in divine philosophy. Therefore, I attempted to make his acquaintance and one day privately asked him, since he knew about Zoroaster and sometimes in his lectures quoted from His writings, whether he had also heard of another Persian Prophet Who had appeared in the second half of the nineteenth century in Iran, and Whose principal teaching was the Unity of Mankind? My elderly professor immediately responded, 'Do you mean the Bahá'í Faith?' Astonished, I agreed, and he asked whether I was a Bahá'í. I replied that I had been born into a Bahá'í family and had declared my faith, and he then stated that he had learned about the Faith in Germany and had read a few books in German and French about it. He also said that he admired the teachings of Bahá'u'lláh and expressed his pleasure in meeting me. I cannot convey how this conversation affected and moved me.

A Holiday in the Caucasus

In 1927, on the invitation of the Spiritual Assembly of Baku, I went to the Caucasus for a teaching trip, and for a period of three months spent my time meeting the Bahá'í friends and seekers of Baku, Gandzha and Tiflis. In Gandzha, I also visited the resting-place of Nizámíy-i-Ganjaví, the eloquent twelfth-century poet of Iran, whose grave was at the time outside the city in the valley of 'Abbás Mírzá* where I said a few prayers. This visit has a story behind it in that for a while I kept asking my host to take me to Nizámí's resting-place, but he, on the grounds that the weather was too hot and the journey too long, would not give me a direct answer. Finally, I decided to go by myself without his help, and rented a carriage to take me there. The carriage driver raised the cover of the carriage to protect me

* He was a general in the one-day Gandzha War which occurred on 25 October 1826.

against the burning sun, but the heat was so bad that I immediately began perspiring all over and thirst overtook me. We passed through the dry desert and after many hours we finally arrived at our destination. In the bottom of a valley there was a ruin, which I was told was the resting-place of Nizámí. I spent a few minutes there and then returned to the city. The wisdom of this trip remained a mystery to my carriage driver, and in fact he did not think that I was quite a sane person to undertake such a journey only to see a ruin, and spend my money for it too! My host was also troubled because of my long absence, and began complaining when I returned. I used my wit and little jokes to comfort him and begged him, instead of complaints, to give me food and water as I had no strength left in me. I later heard that the remains of Nizámí were transferred to the city, a befitting mausoleum was erected on his grave, and his statue was placed in the square of the town.

In the same city, Gandzha, one day my host informed me that the family was going on vacation to a summer camp, and asked me to accompany them. So early one morning we all got up and, after making the necessary preparations, mounted the carriage pulled by two oxen and began our journey. We travelled for two days before we reached the summer camp. On the first day, after a few hours of travelling we stopped at sunset on the slope of a high mountain with snow-covered peaks, and decided to spend the night there. The ladies of the household and the children slept in the carriage and the men spent the night in the fresh air. I covered myself with a thin blanket and in that bitterly cold night lay down on the bare ground, and surprisingly had a very deep sleep! I woke up when the stars were still shining and joined my companions to continue our journey. At sunrise the temperature began to rise and by midday it was so hot that it was almost intolerable. To add to the heat were huge green flies that attacked the poor oxen from every side, and those helpless animals were covered with blood by their bites. After two days we finally arrived at the summer camp of my host, pitched our tents on the slope of a mountain, and after making a fire and eating our dinner retired to our beds in anticipation of the morning's activities. From that morning on all I did was walk in the fresh air, down into the valleys, climbing up the mountains, searching for springs, and picking wild flowers. And more, kebab, whole-wheat bread, yoghurt, and fragrant herbs and vegetables were provided when I returned from my walking expeditions at noon. Alas, that those happy days passed quickly and we had to return to the suffocating environment of the city.

After our return my only consolation was to meet with the Bahá'í friends and seekers in different firesides to discuss the validity of the Cause of God. I also spent some time in Tiflis, the capital of Georgia, and attended many meetings. The seekers of this city, however, were mostly Muslims and I rarely met a native Georgian. This was mostly because the two communities lived in separate quarters and had very little contact with each other.

Also, before leaving for Gandzha and Tiflis, and after my return from these two cities, I met the friends of Baku on numerous occasions, and happy memories of 1924, when I had made my first trip to Baku, vividly returned to mind.

I should like now to return to my memories.

6. I was elected to the Spiritual Assembly of Moscow in 1928, and, on the recommendations of other members, began to hold Bahá'í classes for children and youth. One day I was invited for lunch at the summer home of one of the Bahá'ís, a few miles outside Moscow. Since I had an Assembly meeting that evening, I decided to return to Moscow for it; however, when I arrived at the station, the train had already left and I found that my watch was one

minute slow! There was heavy snow on the ground, and since the next train was not due until three hours later, in my inexperience I decided to walk to Moscow. The snow was up to my knees but, regardless, I began to walk parallel to the railroad. It suffices to say that it was midnight before I reached my room, half-dead, and had to spend the next two days in bed to recover from my exhaustion.

7. In my first year in the university, the students of the Schools of Education, Chemistry and Medicine decided to take a field trip to Astrakhan and visit the Volga River* and its beautiful beaches. Among fifty students I was chosen to be the leader of the group; we took the train to Nizhni-Novgorod (now Gorki), spent the night there, and boarded the ship for Astrakhan in the morning. We had two short stops in Kazan and Saratov before we reached one of the most beautiful ports of the Volga where the ship anchored for five hours to take new passengers aboard and receive additional cargo, and we naturally went ashore by boat to enjoy ourselves in the meantime. When we reached the shore, one of the students announced that there was a village in the vicinity that produced a most famous honey drink, and suggested that we go there and buy some for the remainder of our journey. His suggestion was so warmly received that it was not possible to prevent them from going, and, except for myself and two or three other students, everybody left for the village. We waited for them in vain, and the ship left without us at five in the afternoon. It was not until seven o'clock when they returned, happily laughing and giggling, that I knew the honey drink had done its work and had truly numbed their senses. After a few minutes their laughter was gone and all fell into a deep sleep until after midnight. When at last they regained consciousness, and realized they had missed the ship, they

* The Volga, which flows in the European part of Russia, is one of the largest and longest (about 3,700 kilometres) rivers of Europe. It rises from the headwaters of the Valdai Hills and empties into the Caspian Sea.

began to plead with me to meet with the Director of the port and find a solution to this problem. I made efforts, located the Director and told him our story. He, after much negotiation, and expressing his regret for our lack of discipline, finally agreed to allow us to board the next ship with our same tickets, but told us we were responsible to convince the ship ticket-collector ourselves. We were very thankful that no problems were encountered during the rest of the trip, and we finally reached Astrakhan. We spent three days in that city, went sightseeing, visited all the attractive places, and then returned to Moscow via the same route.

Astrakhan is one of the most important ports of the Volga River, and is located about 100 km. north of the Caspian Sea. Its population was 300,000 at the time, and fishing and its related industries constituted its major commerce. There were, of course, many other established factories and businesses.

8. In my senior year in the university, I accompanied one of my fellow students to Arkhangelsk, located in the extreme north of Russian Europe, to inspect a few schools in fulfilment of university requirements. We left Moscow and travelled by train for two days to a point where we had to continue by sled. Everything was covered in deep snow, and the reflection of the sun was truly blinding. Even the horses had difficulty moving in that snow. I was dressed in a very heavy overcoat, fur hat and winter boots; nevertheless, I could not keep myself warm and almost froze on the way. We finally arrived at a small town and were offered lodging in its school, but neither of us could rest that night because of the severe cold. We spent another day on the way under these conditions, and at last reached a village. Fortunately, we were given a warm room and comfortable accommodation, and had a good sleep that night.

When I awoke in the morning and looked out the window, I saw, to my great astonishment, a group of people who had broken the ice of the river and had immersed themselves up to their chests in that icy water. Habit forms the second nature of human beings, and I could not help but think that if our parents followed the advice of 'Abdu'l-Bahá and guided their children to grow accustomed to hardship,* and did not over-protect them against heat and cold, we would all demonstrate a higher degree of patience and tolerance when facing the difficulties of life. At any rate, we inspected the schools, and after giving a number of lectures on education, which were also a part of our programme, we returned to Moscow.

9. During one of my summer vacations I visited Leningrad. This city, which was the capital of Tsarist Russia, was founded in 1703 by Peter the Great and built in the style of Western European cities on a territory that was forcibly taken from Sweden. The city was very beautiful and had wide streets adorned with lovely houses on both sides. The famous avenue of Neva is truly handsome, and many people from all walks of life come, especially in the evenings, to visit and enjoy it. The renowned literary piece of Gogol, *Nevski Prospekt*, is a poetic description of this avenue. A statue of Peter the Great, mounted on his horse and extending his hand towards the West, is built on the shores of the Gulf of Finland, and attracts many European artists.

I was there during the month of June, and among other tourists used to ride the boat on the Neva River after midnight and read a book or newspaper, as in that part of the world at the beginning of summer there are only a few minutes between sunset and sunrise. I wish I were an artist or a poet so that I could describe befittingly the beauties of that river and its shores, but unfortunately I can only list interesting features and leave it at that.

* 'Bring them up to work and strive, and accustom them to hardship.' (*Selections from the Writings of 'Abdu'l-Bahá*, p. 129.)

One of the God-given beauties of Leningrad is the area around the Neva River. This river, 75 km. long, flows from the south-west corner of Lake Ladoga into the Gulf of Finland, and then into the Baltic Sea. It freezes early in December and melts in mid-April.

Included in the fine buildings that are visited by every tourist are the Hermitage, Winter Palace, Peter and Paul fortress, Pushkin, and many others. In the Hermitage museum a number of rooms have been appropriated to Persian art, where carpet-weaving, sword-making, inlaid works and cloths woven with gold in ancient and modern Persia have been put on view in a most exquisite way. I also visited the resting-place of Tchaikovsky, the famous Russian composer, and then at the conclusion of my vacation returned to Moscow.

10. In 1927 I decided to visit the palaces of the Kremlin, which at the time required special permission. The Kremlin is the nucleus of Moscow, and is one of the most beautiful structures in the world. The citadel was initially built of wood in AD 1156; the wall was later replaced with white stones and red bricks some time between 1485 and 1495, and gradually it assumed its present form. Its exquisite towers were added in the seventeenth century. Within the citadel of the Kremlin there are several cathedrals, palaces, and a number of museums, each well known in the world.

One of the interesting features of the Kremlin is its 'King of all Bells', an enormous bell made of bronze during the period 1733–5. It weighs 200 tons and is seven metres high. When it was being installed in 1737, it fell and a piece weighing 12 tons broke away. Through this crack tourists are able to enter the bell. Another is the huge cannon, made also of bronze in 1588. It weighs about 40 tons and has a five-metre-long barrel with 89-cm. calibre. This cannon is preserved to this day.

11. From the very beginning, and as I became familiar

with the Russian language, I was deeply interested in the writings of Tolstoy and always wished to visit his resting-place, especially as this prominent author praised the Faith and 'Abdu'l-Bahá revealed a Tablet in his honour.

During one of my university years I took the train to Tula, and then from there went by carriage and on foot to Yasnaya Polyana, the birthplace and residence of Leo Tolstoy, where he is also buried. I visited his grave, which is enclosed within a wooden wall, and, as I had wished, said a few prayers. I also visited his museum, in which the original manuscript of his masterpiece, *War and Peace*, is kept. Very happy that I had made the trip, I returned to Moscow.

12. I have precious recollections of Bahá'í administrative institutions and the condition of the Faith in Moscow, but since a detailed account will be tiresome, only a brief review will be given.

The Spiritual Assembly of Moscow and its committees met regularly. The Bahá'í children met once a week to attend the Bahá'í classes and also to receive instruction in the Persian language. There were also Bahá'í meetings in which, after prayers were read, a speaker would give a talk and highlight the principal teachings of the Faith. A special spirit and radiance always governed these meetings.

While in Moscow I naturally took advantage of its literary, scientific, and artistic centres, and attended, and profoundly enjoyed, many of its fine theatres and opera houses.

In the spring of 1930 I completed my studies in Psychology and Education, and with the guidance of a number of my professors wrote my thesis on one of the important aspects of education, which was fortunately accepted and praised by the designated committee. It was published in the official journal of the Ministry of Education, and I even received a sum of money as royalty. Attached to my degree was a certificate which stated, ''Alí-Akbar-i-Furútan has proved himself to be a very active, serious, and conscientious student during his years of study in the University, and has shown special interest in mastering methods of teaching a mother tongue . . . '

I can attribute my success in the university to the prayer of the beloved Guardian: ' . . . This servant in this illumined spot prays at the sacred Threshold from the depth of his heart for your peace of mind, prosperity and success, so that you may excel in divine knowledge and material learning . . .'

4

Return to Iran

After completion of my studies, because of my numerous Bahá'í activities the Government decided that I should leave that country and return to my native land. Therefore, after sixteen years in Russia, I returned to Iran via 'Ishqábád and Baku and reached Bandar-Anzali. A few friends, two of whom I already knew, greeted me, and I began my activities in Iran.

The Bahá'ís of this port, and later those in Rasht, were very kind to me and I continually gave talks in various meetings, held Bahá'í classes and went on teaching trips to Bahá'í centres in the province of Gílán. It was during this period that I wrote an article for *Parvarish*, a newspaper in Rasht, and it was favourably received.

I went to Tehran from Rasht, and attended the Convention. (In those days no national conventions were held.) The Ḥaẓíratu'l-Quds of Tehran was, at the time, outside the Yúsif-Ábád gate, in an area known as 'Bagh-i-Mujallah'. Twenty-five delegates were present, and Mírzá Muḥammad-i-Partuvi, the only person I knew, introduced me. Then a radiant believer with half-grey hair, whom I later found to be Jináb-i-Valíyu'llah-i-Varqá, the chairman of the Convention, said that the delegates had reached the decision in my absence to offer me either to stay in Tehran and, with the help of a few prominent Bahá'ís who were holding important positions in the Ministry of Education, become an employee of the Government, or go to the Ádharbáyján province as a travelling teacher. As my father had willed, I preferred to go into the teaching field and this decision was much praised by the delegates. In the same meeting I also gave an account of the Bahá'í activities and condition of the friends in Russia, which received enthusiastic attention.

After a few days, together with Mírzá 'Anáyatu'lláh Aḥmadpúr-i-Mílání, the delegate from Ádharbáyján, we went to Tabríz. We had to ride the outdated and ancient buses available at the time, passed through Qazvin, Zanján, Míyánaj, and Básminj, and the terrifying passes of Qáflánkúh and Shiblí, and finally reached Tabríz. My activities began at once and included:

1. Holding firesides for seekers in the homes of the friends
2. Organizing Bahá'í meetings in the Ḥaẓíratu'l-Quds
3. Beginning large-scale Friday meetings for non-Bahá'ís
4. Organizing Bahá'í classes for children and youth
5. Beginning separate classes for Bahá'í women

During this period I received another letter from the beloved Guardian dated 11 May 1930.

The detailed report of that beloved friend, which contained the news of Bahá'í activities in Russia, reached the most holy presence of the Guardian . . . The report was comprehensive and complete, and was acceptable in his sight. He expressed his favour and grace, and praised and admired your . . . perseverance, and devotion. It is certain that the manifestation of these divine sentiments . . . will increase your spiritual strength, will further your devotion, will bring joy and happiness to your heart and soul, and that the afflictions and sorrows which you have encountered will be removed and forgotten.

And in the margin, in the blessed handwriting of the Guardian:

O spiritual Friend:

Do not be vexed and discouraged because of the present difficulties . . . Patience and forbearance are necessary. He verily strengthens the weak with His almighty power, and shall render His loved ones victorious through the holy souls of the Kingdom of Abhá. For the present time, you should engage in Bahá'í services in Iran . . .

The servant of His Threshold,
Shoghi

The following are a few recollections of my sojourn in Á<u>dh</u>arbáyján:

1. I was informed one day that one of the divines of the city, together with a few of his companions, had decided to come and see me, and they were on their way. At the appointed time, a handsome man with a black beard and wearing a cloak arrived. He was accompanied by ten others. After exchanging the customary pleasantries, the divine told me that he had come to discuss the Bahá'í Faith, and stated that he wished to record our conversation for future publication so that readers might judge who was right and who wrong. I answered that investigation of truth did not require these formalities, and efforts put forth in the path of God did not call for arguments or strife. The verses of God, I stated, and the traditions of the Imams could alone be a valid measuring-stick by which truth could be separated from falsehood, and I suggested that we both resort to these means and in all sincerity cling to the cord of wisdom and prudence. (See Qur'án XVI: 126.)

He refused my suggestion and, persisting in his idea, instructed one of his companions to record our conversation. He then suddenly asked me, 'What was the miracle of Bahá'u'lláh, Whom you claim to be the Promised One of Islam?' I replied, 'What was the miracle of the Prophet of Islam in Whom you have professed your belief?' He said, 'The Seal of the Prophets had many miracles, but should you decide to attribute a miracle to Bahá'u'lláh, I would refuse it as I have seen your books and have especially read Abu'l-Faḍl-i-Gulpáygání's *Fará'id*, and know that you do not accept the miracles of the Prophets.' I told him that the Qur'án would be the judge between him and me, that if he found one verse in the Book of God which testified to performing a miracle I would unhesitatingly and immediately accept all his claims. I then recited the following verse from the Sura, 'The Children of Israel', in which it was revealed:

And they say, 'By no means will we believe on thee till thou cause a fountain to gush forth for us from the earth; or, till thou have a garden of palm-trees and grapes, and thou cause forth-gushing rivers to gush forth in its midst; or thou make the heaven to fall on us, as thou hast given out, in pieces; or thou bring God and the angels to vouch for thee; or thou have a house of gold; or thou mount up into Heaven; nor will we believe in thy mounting up, till thou send down to us a book which we may read.' Say: Praise be to my Lord! Am I more than a man, an apostle? (Qur'án XVII: 92–5.)

I then added, 'You surely know that God in the Qur'án has refuted miracles and has only ordained the revealed verses to be the standard of truth.' The divine replied that one could not believe in a Prophet Who had not performed a miracle, and asked me to prove the truth of the Prophethood of Muḥammad without referring to His miracles!

We continued in this argumentative manner for five hours, but reached no positive conclusion. At the end of our discussion we were quite tired, and he, finding no other point to argue about, asked me why, if my religion was truly from God, Avárih had left the Bahá'í Faith? I replied that his argument was futile as after the passing of Muḥammad many of His followers did the same,* and reminded him of Judas, one of the disciples of Christ who betrayed Him for thirty pieces of silver. (See *Selections from the Writings of 'Abdu'l-Bahá*, p. 212.) At last, in the evening they departed, leaving me totally exhausted. I saw this divine on the streets several times later, but we passed each other without entering into conversation.

* 'After the ascension of Muḥammad, . . . the tribes around Medina apostatized from their Faith, turning back to the idolatry of pagan times.' ('Abdu'l-Bahá, *The Secret of Divine Civilization*, p. 44.)

2. One day one of the natives of Tabríz came to our house, and we were told that he was a former Muslim who had been converted to Christianity by the missionaries. He continued to visit us for a while, and one day he confided to me that he was actually an atheist at heart, and even though he had become a Christian he still did not believe in God, or in His Prophets. He then suggested that if the Bahá'ís paid him more money than the Christians, he would again change his religion and become a Bahá'í, and would even assist in teaching and spreading the Cause! I expressed my appreciation for his frankness, but stated that the Bahá'í communities did not need or wish to resort to such means to spread the Cause of God, and recommended that he be honest with his co-religionists and tell them the truth. He smiled and said his stomach needed food, and the food had to be provided one way or another!

A few days passed, until he once again came to say that the minister of his church with the church custodian, who was also formerly a Muslim and had become a Christian, wanted to see me. We made an appointment, and the minister and the custodian, 'Abdu'lláh, arrived. The minister said that 'Abdu'lláh wanted to discuss the Bahá'í Faith with me, indicating that he himself did not consider me worthy to engage in discussion with him.

I asked 'Abdu'lláh, 'Have you become a Christian now?' 'Yes,' he replied. I asked, 'What was your former religion?' He answered, 'I was a Muslim.' 'Did you not accept Christ when you were a Muslim,' I enquired, 'as according to the text of the Qur'án each Muslim should testify to the truth of the revelation of Christ and accept the Bible?' The minister hastily interfered at this point: "Abdu'lláh means that now that he has become a Christian, he denies Muḥammad.' 'Abdu'lláh confirmed this statement. 'What was your reason for denying Muḥammad?' I asked. He repeated the usual accusations of Christian missionaries against

Muḥammad. I answered each of these in simple language, referring to the verses of the Old and New Testaments. 'Abdu'lláh was startled and, after listening to me, addressed the minister: 'Why have you not told me these facts before?' The minister interrupted him: 'How can Muḥammad be a Prophet when He has brought no proof except His sword and has said, "I am a Prophet by the sword,"* while Christ is the Prince of Peace?' I answered, 'You read the Bible by day and by night, and how is it that you have not noted chapter 10, verses 34 and 35 of the Gospel of Matthew in which the Christ has said, "Think not that I am come to send peace on earth: I came not to send peace, but a sword. For I am come to set a man at variance against his father, and the daughter against her mother, and the daughter-in-law against her mother-in-law."' I also mentioned chapter 22, verse 36 of the Gospel of Luke, in which Christ has said, 'But now, . . . he that hath no sword, let him sell his garment, and buy one.' And verse 38 of the same chapter, 'And they said, Lord, behold, here are two swords . . .'

'Abdu'lláh, although illiterate, sensed that the minister had misled him, that whatever he had said about Muḥammad was true also of Christ, and he converted back to Islam in the same meeting! The minister naturally became extremely angry and at once left us.

3. In the beginning of 1930 I left Tabríz to visit the friends of Riḍá'íyyih (Urúmíyyih), and with the approval of the Spiritual Assembly of that city, decided to meet the Education Superintendent who had heard about me. He warmly greeted me, and in the course of our friendly conversation asked me to arrange educational conferences for the teachers and students of Riḍá'íyyih as I had done in Tabríz.

Three meetings were arranged in the assembly hall of the secondary school, and my talks were enthusiastically

* *The Secret of Divine Civilization*, p. 43, a tradition of Muḥammad.

received by the audience. In our fourth meeting, however, a certain teacher, who was from Tehran and taught French, left his seat and angrily began to criticize the audience for listening to, and admiring, someone who was known to belong to a 'certain community'. His protest was given with such vehemence, and his statements about my relation to a 'certain community' were so vague and confusing that the audience began to show signs of discomfort and anxiety. I did not lose any time and addressed them, saying, 'Do you know what "a certain community" means? The gentleman wants to say that I am a Bahá'í, but does not have the courage to be direct.' I added that I had never intended to conceal my beliefs from anyone, but that my educational lectures were not connected with my religion. I also explained that the teachings of the Bahá'í Faith, whose purpose was to establish the unity of mankind, were designed to bring peace rather than harm to the country and its people. After the conclusion of this meeting a group of teachers and students approached me and expressed their regret for what had happened.

The news of this incident was spread in the city, and when *Riḍá'íyyih*, the local newspaper, published a summary of my talk, I began to receive threatening messages from the merchants of the city that I should leave as soon as possible or face grave consequences. After a while, again with the approval of the Spiritual Assembly and with permission from the police authorities, I held a conference in the only cinema on the harmful effects of alcohol and drugs. This meeting was advertised in the daily newspapers, and such a huge crowd attended that the police had difficulty in maintaining order. After the talk, while leaving the theatre, the Chief of Police, a handsome and courteous young man, approached and advised me that I had better leave the town, as it was in a state of commotion and the possibility of unwholesome events existed.

On the instruction of the Spiritual Assembly I left Riḍá'íyyih immediately, spent the night with one of the Bahá'ís in a nearby village, and returned to Tabríz the next day.

Saysán and its Bahá'í Schools

During the last months of 1931, on the instructions of the beloved Guardian, Effie Baker came to Tabríz to photograph the historical and holy places of the Faith in that city, and my wife Ataieh and I accompanied her to Saysán. From there, we wrote a letter to the beloved Guardian and asked permission to transfer to Saysán and establish a Bahá'í school for girls and boys. After two months we received his response in which, among other points, his secretary wrote on his behalf:

> . . . You have written regarding the arrangement for the school in Saysán, and the education of the Bahá'í children there, saying that you and your respected wife, 'Aṭá'íyyih [Ataieh], intended to undertake this project for a time, and to render the worthy service of teaching the children, fostering education, enlightening minds and perfecting the knowledge of others. This intention was accepted and approved and is appreciated by the beloved Guardian, and he stated that it is certain that you will be confirmed and will meet with success . . . This letter was written on the instructions of the beloved Guardian. (16 Sharaf 89, 15 January 1933.)

Soon after receiving this letter I received a cable from the Central Assembly for Iran* urgently summoning me to Tehran. It was winter time, the weather was very cold, and the roads were closed because of the snow. All the travel agencies I referred to gave a negative response, but on the suggestion of one of them, I decided to ride an oil tanker to Tehran! We had driven only a few kilometres out of Tabríz when we were stranded in snow and had to stop.

* In those days the Local Spiritual Assembly of Tehran acted as the Central Assembly for Iran.

Fortunately, there was a little roadside café in the vicinity and we took refuge there, but it was so crowded that we had to stand all night. The snow finally stopped, the roads were opened and we continued our journey. It took us four days to travel the distance between Tabríz and Tehran, but upon my arrival I immediately reported to the Assembly. I was told that I had been appointed principal of the Tarbíyat School (a Bahá'í school for boys). However, when the instructions of the beloved Guardian were conveyed to them, they decided to postpone the appointment and I returned to Tabríz.

There, I began making the necessary preparations for our move to Saysán, and after saying farewell to the members of the Spiritual Assembly and friends of Tabríz, together with my wife and our fourteen-day-old child, I rented a carriage and we began our journey to Saysán. We were greeted by the members of the Spiritual Assembly of Saysán and a few of the friends there, and were taken to the Ḥaẓíratu'l-Quds where a room was given to us for our accommodation.

With the assistance of the Bahá'ís, the building of the school was soon completed, and about 700 students, boys and girls, began their education. In an amazingly short time, the students demonstrated magnificent progress in all their work, to such a degree that when the well-known Bahá'í teacher, Mrs Keith Ransom-Kehler came to Saysán, she expressed her great admiration of the school and its students, and later published an article to this effect in one of the Bahá'í magazines.

At the end of the academic year I sent a report to the beloved Guardian concerning the Bahá'í activities in Saysán, to which I received the following response:

15 Sharaf 90 [14 January 1934]

Your comprehensive and refreshing report of Masá'il 90, on the condition of the Bahá'ís in Saysán, the detailed account of the repairs done on the Ḥaẓíratu'l-Quds, the establishment of the schools for boys and for girls, and the other Bahá'í institutions and activities, was received in the holy presence of the Guardian of the Cause of God . . . and brought much joy and happiness to his heart . . . He instructed me to write the following: the noble efforts of that worthy servant will not be forgotten. It is hoped that in the future, in the capital of the country, you will succeed in rendering greater services, and will perform more glorious feats . . . The arena of service will be unboundedly vast in the future. Please God that you may also be confirmed and honoured to render international services . . .

In the margin, in the handwriting of the beloved Guardian:

O thou loving Friend:

May God confirm you and increase your honour and glory in your efforts to serve His Cause and exalt His Faith. May He fulfil your heart's desire through His mercy and bounty, and His might and grace.

Now, a few lines will be written about the village of Saysán, which is located on the slope of Sahand mountain. It has a pleasant summer, but its winter is very severe and cold, especially for those who are not from that area. Sometimes the snowfall is so extensive that it buries the houses, and people have to make tunnels through the snow to be able to leave and take care of their needs. Agricultural produce such as wheat, barley, and potatoes is its major source of income, but carpet-weaving and jájím-making (jájím is a coarse, woollen cloth used for bedding, or as a carpet) are also popular in Saysán. Cattle and sheep raising are very limited. The Cause of God was first introduced in Saysán during the time of the Báb, and a great number of S͟hayk͟hís became Bábís. They were also firm believers when the sun of the Blessed Beauty rose, and many Tablets have been issued in their honour from His Most Exalted Pen. The following is one of these Tablets from Bahá'u'lláh, addressed to the Bahá'ís of Saysán:

In the Name of Him Who is the All-Seeing, the Incomparable. Unto the friends of Saysán the glad-tidings of the favour of God the Compassionate are announced. All are, and have been, under the gaze of His tender mercy, and have found their refuge beneath the shadow of God's towering Lote Tree. Meditate upon the divine grace. The divines of the world who consider themselves the most learned, the most erudite, the most scholarly, and the most eminent amongst the peoples of the earth, have not attained to one drop from the ocean of His Utterance, nor have they been honoured with the slightest mention in the presence of the Merciful Lord. Ye, however, by the grace of God, exalted be His glory, have attained to such a station that the Pen of the Most High in the Most Great Prison is remembering you. Exalted is this high, this supreme station, and this lofty, this most mighty Remembrance.

A few of the Bahá'ís of Saysán had the honour of attaining the presence of Bahá'u'lláh in the prison-city of 'Akká. A few others, after the ascension of the Blessed Beauty, visited 'Abdu'l-Bahá, and certain ones were fortunate enough to serve in the Holy Land during the ministry of the Guardian. The friends of Saysán have always been very devoted, self-sacrificing, courageous and inflamed with the love of God, and to the best of their ability have extended continually their protection to the oppressed Bahá'ís of the neighbouring villages.

Many of the early Bahá'ís and teachers of the Cause including Áqá Mírzá Ḥusayn-i-Zanjání, Áqá Shaykh Aḥmad-i-Mu'allim-i-Uskú'í, and Áqá Siyyid Asadu'lláh-i-Qumí from the East, and the immortal Martha Root, Mrs Keith Ransom-Kehler and others from the West have stopped in this village and, in their memoirs, have given accounts of their meetings with the friends of Saysán.

The first National Spiritual Assembly of the Bahá'ís of Iran was elected at the close of ASH 1312 (early 1934), and for the first time all the local communities elected their delegates to the National Convention in Tehran. I was elected as one of the delegates from the province of Ádharbáyján, and left Saysán for Tehran a few days before the Convention. A few years had to elapse before I was again given a chance to revisit Saysán.

The Tarbíyat Schools for Boys and Girls

This first National Convention of the Bahá'ís of Iran was held in the National Ḥaẓíratu'l-Quds during the festival of Riḍván. Ninety-five delegates came from every corner of the country and, after consultation, elected the National Spiritual Assembly. Much to my surprise, I was one of the elected members, and later, in our first meeting, I was also elected secretary of the Assembly. During the same year, following the Guardian's instructions in his letter of 5 March 1933 addressed to the Central Assembly of Iran, I was appointed principal of Tarbíyat School, and moved to Tehran to take up this important task.

The all-boys' Tarbíyat School was founded during the ministry of 'Abdu'l-Bahá in AD 1900 through the devoted efforts of a number of the learned and well-known Bahá'ís such as Hand of the Cause of God Mírzá Muḥammad-Ḥasan-i-Adíb, Hand of the Cause of God Mírzá Muḥammad-Taqíy-i-Ibn-i-Abhar, Dr Muḥammad Khán-i-Munajjim, Dr 'Aṭá'u'lláh Bakhsháyish and Áṣifu'l-Ḥukamá. With ceaseless encouragement and the favours of the Centre of the Covenant, and with the toil and diligence of its board of directors and of such sanctified souls as Muḥammad-'Alí Khán-i-Bahá'í and Mírzá Yúsif Khán-i-Vujdání, the school gradually added to its prestige and fame. It should be mentioned that a few American believers also put forth sacrificial efforts in promoting the interests and advancement of that institution.

The Master, 'Abdu'l-Bahá, has written many Tablets in honour of the administrators of this school, from which the following lines are taken:

It is the wish of this servant that this school may gradually excel all the schools of the world. (*To Muḥammad-'Alí Khán-i-Bahá'í.*)

The hope is cherished that the Tarbíyat School may attain such a degree of excellence that the Bahá'í children will no longer have to go to Europe and bear the burden of considerable expense. (*To members of Tarbíyat Schools Committee.*)

My hope is that the Tarbíyat School may be under the protection of the One True God, and may achieve extraordinary progress. (*To Hand of the Cause Ibn-i-Abhar.*)

I replaced Mírzá 'Azízu'lláh Miṣbáḥ who for many years was a professor and the principal of the school, but because of poor eyesight was no longer able to continue his meritorious services. There were about 600 Bahá'í and non-Bahá'í students attending at the time, and all the teachers, with the exception of two or three, were Bahá'ís. The board of directors of Tarbíyat School, its principal and all its teachers and staff members exerted their utmost efforts to administer the affairs of the school in a Bahá'í fashion, and employed every available means to further the progress of the students, that its good name and prestige might be kept intact.

The National Spiritual Assembly had in mind that the Tarbíyat Schools, which were exclusively owned and controlled by the Faith, must not remain open on Bahá'í Holy Days. To observe this sacred duty to cease work on the Holy Days, which is the spiritual and moral obligation of every Bahá'í, the National Spiritual Assembly issued an explicit instruction to the board of directors and principal of the school to close the two Bahá'í schools (for boys and girls) on the anniversary of the Martyrdom of the Báb, and to explain this action to the authorities sufficiently to prevent any misunderstanding on their part.

Dr Youness Khan-i-Afrukhtih, a member of the National Assembly, and I went to the Ministry of Education, and gave to the Deputy Minister a full explanation of the beliefs of Bahá'ís and their moral obligation to observe the nine Holy Days. He, however, did not agree to recognize the Holy Days, and our future meetings were also of no avail.

On 6 December 1934, in observance of the anniversary of the Martyrdom of the Báb, the school was, of course, closed. (In Iran this anniversary was observed according to the lunar calendar.) On the following Saturday the students resumed their normal schedule, but on the same day we received the following letter from the Ministry of Education:

17 Á<u>dh</u>ar 1313 [8 December 1934]
. . . The Ministry of Education hereby nullifies the license of that school, which was issued on 26/3/10 [17 June 1931]. As of this date, you are no longer permitted to operate this high school.

(signed and sealed)
'Alí-Aṣ<u>gh</u>ar Ḥikmat
Deputy, Ministry of Education

Our school was closed in this manner.

The all-girls' Tarbíyat School also met with the same fate. This school was founded in 1912 through the efforts of such blessed people as Dr Susan I. Moody and Dr 'Aṭá'u'lláh Ba<u>kh</u><u>sh</u>áyi<u>sh</u>, under the supervision of the Tarbíyat Schools Committee and with official permission of the Government. Many Western and Eastern believers including Miss Lillian Kappes, Dr Genevieve Coy, Mrs Vafá'íyyih Midḥat and Rúḥangíz <u>Kh</u>ánum-i-Fatḥ-'Aẓam and others were among the teaching staff of this institution. Miss Adelaide Sharp, one of the self-sacrificing believers of California, served as the principal of the school from 1929 through 1934, when it was closed. During the same year the Ministry of Education also moved to close all other Bahá'í schools in different parts of the country.

The beloved Guardian has given the following account in *God Passes By*:

. . . at a time when state schools and colleges were practically non-existent in that country, and when the education given in existing religious institutions was lamentably defective, . . . its earliest schools were established, beginning with the Tarbíyat schools in Ṭihrán for both boys and girls, and followed by the Ta'yíd and Mawhibat schools in Hamadán, the Vaḥdat-i-Bashar school in Káshán and other similar educational institutions in Bárfurúsh [Bábul] and Qazvín . . . (p. 299.)

The closing of all schools belonging to the Bahá'í community in that country, as a direct consequence of the refusal of the representatives of that community to permit official Bahá'í institutions, owned and entirely controlled by them, to transgress the clearly revealed law requiring the suspension of work on Bahá'í Holy Days . . . may be regarded as [one of] the initial attempts made in that country whose soil had already been imbued with the blood of countless Bahá'í martyrs, to resist the rise, and frustrate the struggle for the emancipation, of a nascent Administrative Order, whose very roots have sucked their strength from such heroic sacrifice. (p. 363.)

Recollections and Dreams

Now I would like to recount a few of my recollections of those days in Iran:

1. In 1943 I had the privilege of visiting the blessed House of the Báb in Shíráz for the first time. When I first beheld the indescribable view of the city of God from a distance, my heart began pounding and an incredible happiness filled my soul. Passing through the narrow alleys of Shamshírgarhá, the early history of the Faith, its terrible and astonishing events, and the sufferings and martyrdom of the Báb and His zealous followers came vividly to mind. In such a state, and in the company of Afnáns, barefooted, I entered the courtyard of that blessed House. When I inhaled the fragrance of the orange tree planted by the Báb Himself, and saw the well, which had been kept in its original condition, I was immersed in such an ocean of joy and

ecstasy that it cannot be adequately described to others.

After prostrating myself humbly, I climbed the staircase to the upper chamber of that House, the goal of the hearts around which the denizens of the Pavilion of Grandeur circle in adoration.* I lost my control when I entered that sanctified chamber and remembered the glorious night of the Declaration of the Báb to Mullá Ḥusayn, and wept with such a weeping that all those who were with me were also deeply moved. After a while I regained my peace and consoled my soul by reading the Tablet of Visitation and other prayers. Then in utmost humility, lowliness and submission I left the chamber and joined the rest of the pilgrims in the neighbouring courtyard where Mr Afnán showered me with his kindness.

During this journey I also visited the beloved friends of Ábádih, Yazd, Iṣfahán and Dihbíd. In Yazd, in whatever house I entered, I heard tales of the martyrdoms of heroic early believers. Praise God that the Bahá'ís of Yazd, one and all, are the deserving descendants of their lion-hearted ancestors. A spirit of utmost sacrifice was always present in the meetings they held.

In Iṣfahán I visited the house of the Imám-Jum'ih and the illumined residences of the King of Martyrs and the Beloved of Martyrs, in addition to other Bahá'í historical places. In Ábádih I went to Ḥadíqatu'l-Raḥmán, where the heads of the martyrs of Nayríz are buried, and then with my soul nourished to its core returned to Tehran.

2. I was secretary of both the National Spiritual Assembly of Iran and the Local Spiritual Assembly of Tehran, and my responsibilities, in view of my poor health, were a little overwhelming. One day as I was preparing to go to my office, I felt a serious weakness in my body. A physician

* '. . . this is the Spot before which bow down in adoration all the denizens of His kingdom and beyond them the inhabitants of the realm of creation.' (Bahá'u'lláh in *Súriy-i-Ḥajj*.)

was called who diagnosed measles, but as I showed no signs of recovery at home, I was transferred to the hospital. Fifty days passed and fever still persisted, for at that time there were no antibiotics available and treatment of such diseases usually took a long time. One night, however, I had a dream of the beloved Guardian. He had a flower in his hand and had come to visit me. I tried to stand up in respect, but weakness overtook me and I failed in my effort. He said, 'I have brought you this flower.' I took the flower, inhaled its fragrance, kissed it, poured some water from a crystal jug beside my bed into a glass, and put that flower, which had three buds, in the glass. Then the beloved Guardian disappeared. I remember having told myself in my dream that attaining the presence of the Guardian meant health and recovery, and the three buds indicated that after three days my fever would break. On the following evening, the nurse came and took my temperature and gave me the good news that the fever had finally broken after fifty days! I should mention that a few days before the dream I was given a message from the beloved Guardian in which he assured me of his fervent prayers and asked me to cable news of my recovery. Three days after the dream I was able once again to sit on my bed and began eating simple foods. I gradually regained my health and was discharged.

3. I had heard in Baku in earlier years that a certain Mírzá 'Alí-Akbar-i-Ardibílí had written in a Turkish dialect a book against the Faith named *Uṣúl'u-Dín-i-'Avámí* (Principles of Faith for the common people). I had heard also that this book was filled with accusations and calumnies against the Cause of God, although to the credit of its author it had an extremely unworthy introduction aimed at proving the existence of God!

In 1930 when I went to Tabríz, I tried to locate this book, and after much search one of the Bahá'í friends of Ardibíl found a copy and sent it to me in Tabríz. Upon reading it, I saw with my own eyes that what I had heard about it in Baku was entirely true. The humorous point, however, was that its author had applied his seal to the last page of his book to preserve its authenticity, and its publisher had added a note assuring readers that 'Whoever keeps a copy of this excellent book will be protected against the punishments of the Day of Resurrection!'

A few years passed, and I was transferred to Tehran in 1934. One night in a fireside meeting one of the Bahá'ís brought a seeker with him. When he introduced himself, much to my surprise I found that he was a nephew of the same Mírzá 'Alí-Akbar-i-Ardibílí. I asked him whether he had read or seen any of the publications of his uncle. He said that he had not. I related to him briefly the contents of *Uṣúl'u-Dín-i-'Avámí*, and specifically mentioned its introduction. He strongly refused to accept that his uncle had written this book, and considered my comments as insults to the religious rank of his uncle. I told him that I had that book in my possession, and could prove what I had said if he would come to our next meeting. He repeated his certainty that such idle statements could not possibly have been made by his learned uncle, and promised that if I gave him the book he would return my favour with a very precious gift. We made an appointment, and when we met again I gave him the book. He inspected it carefully and when he saw the seal of his uncle on the last page, blood rushed to his face and he told me that I had won! He then gave me a letter as his gift. Opening it, I recognized the handwriting of Ṭáhirih. My joy was such that he noticed it, and assured me repeatedly that the letter was a gift to me. I told him that this gift was indeed precious and asked how he had come to possess it. He said that two of his co-students were close relatives of Ṭáhirih, and they had given him that letter because they believed it had not brought good fortune to their home! The next evening I gave the letter to Jináb-i-

Fáḍil-i-Mázindarání, one of the prominent scholars of Persia, and he confirmed the handwriting of Ṭáhirih. I made a facsimile for him, and sent the original letter to the beloved Guardian.

During my first pilgrimage to the Holy Land in 1941 I saw the letter in the archives, preserved in a beautiful frame, with my name mentioned as its contributor. Now this letter is kept in the International Bahá'í Archives on Mount Carmel, and was acknowledged by the Guardian in his letter addressed to the National Spiritual Assembly of Iran, 16 April 1941.

I have had two dreams which, in my humble opinion, are worthy to be mentioned here:

1. I dreamt that I was in a very large square holding a beautiful mantle in my hand. I knew that the mantle belonged to the Blessed Beauty, Bahá'u'lláh. Suddenly a huge crowd filled the square and all their hands stretched towards me, asking me to give them the mantle. I had no guarantee that they would return it if I gave it to them, and I also knew that if I refused, they would take it by force. Then I saw an ornamented rod left on a stool. I picked it up, hung the mantle on the rod and told the anxious crowd that I would raise the rod so that everybody could see it. As soon as I did this, the rod grew taller and began to ascend swiftly into space. As everybody was watching, suddenly the Blessed Beauty appeared within the mantle and graciously began to walk over the clouds. A gentle breeze was wafting, moving His jet-black hair which was spread over His shoulders. I cried, 'O people! Blessed are ye, for ye see His Countenance. Blessed are ye!'

I woke up with my own cry. It was dawn and I was in my bed.

2. At another time I dreamt that I was the servant of the Báb, and only thirteen years old. The Báb was in prison in a

building in the middle of a large garden. Trees had overcrowded the garden, and a muddy stream passed through it. The walls around the garden were half-destroyed. The building consisted of a small room and a larger hall, and one had to climb ten or twelve steps to enter it. The hall was carpeted and had large stained-glass windows through which the sun shone in. At the head of the hall there were a few mattresses with pillows, and close to the door, on a small table, were a brass jug and basin. (These details are printed so vividly in my mind that I feel I have seen the building several times while awake.)

I knew we were in Máh-kú and that the Báb was in prison. He was sitting at the head of the room, and I, with my hands crossed in front of me as a sign of reverence, was in His presence. Since there was absolute silence, I took advantage of the opportunity and asked, 'My Beloved, what is the purpose of the revelation of the Bayán?' He answered, 'Him Whom God shall make Manifest.' I asked, 'To whom do all these prayers that Thou hast revealed belong?' He stated, 'They are revealed to testify to the attributes and virtues of Him Whom God shall make Manifest.' I asked, 'Hast Thou met Bahá'u'lláh?' He looked firmly at me and asked, 'What day is today?' I answered, 'It is Friday.' (When I awoke I realized it was Sunday.) He said, 'I suspend work on Fridays and do not answer questions.' I said, 'My Beloved, the air is pleasant today and the meadow is green; wouldst Thou roam around outside?' He replied, 'Are We not a Prisoner, and are not guards on watch?' I looked outside and saw the guard with his rifle. At this time He arose and stated, 'I wish to perform my ablutions. Do We have water?' I immediately took a container and rushed down the stairs to get some water from the muddy stream. When I returned I saw that the Báb, that Exalted One, had performed His ablutions with the little water left in the basin, and that water was still dripping from His beard. I went to one side so that He could say His prayers, and then I awoke. It was still dark and the stars were shining brilliantly. I left my bed, performed my ablutions, and engaged in prayer.

5

First Pilgrimage to the Holy Land

Early in 1941, during the Second World War, means were miraculously provided for me and my family to go on pilgrimage. In the company of my mother, my wife, and my eight-year-old daughter, together with other pilgrims, we set out on our journey. Passing through Qazvin, Hamadan, Kermanshah and Qasr-i-Shirin, we reached Baghdad. We stayed for two days in that historical city, holy to Bahá'ís, and met with the friends there. Then via Rutbah, we arrived at Ẓemakh, which was then on the border of Palestine. Our luggage was inspected at the border, and since we carried two very expensive silk rugs, which were the gift of a believer, we were asked to pay a considerable amount of duty. However, when we explained that these rugs were brought for the House of 'Abdu'l-Bahá, they were released without charge. The director of Customs, who was Christian and a handsome and courteous man, happened to travel in the same bus with us to Haifa, and asked me about the value of the rugs. I said that I did not know as they were the gift of another believer. He offered to pay me an equivalent amount for an identical pair if I would promise to buy and send them to him in Ẓemakh on my return to Iran. I had to excuse myself from accepting this responsibility while the War was continuing, explaining that I had no experience in these affairs. He said that he would trust me with such a large amount only because I was a Bahá'í and could not understand why I refused his request. I replied that I had to excuse myself precisely because I was a Bahá'í! When we reached Haifa we parted as friends.

It was during late afternoon of Sunday, 16 February 1941, when we set foot in the garden of the House of 'Abdu'l-Bahá in the illumined city of Haifa, passing through a gate marked by a brass plate with ''Abdu'l-Bahá 'Abbás' beautifully engraved on it. The ladies of our pilgrimage group were guided inside by a believer, and the men were taken to a large basement. A radiant old man, wearing a long black cloak and a Persian head-dress, similar to a Turkish fez, was sitting on the divan (*mandar*). After exchanging pleasantries, he wrote our names on a piece of paper and left the room. He returned in a few minutes and announced that the beloved Guardian was prepared to receive us, and guided us to the upper floor. I cannot convey my feelings in those moments. The ecstasy of meeting the Guardian filled my soul, and my impatient heart was beating so hard that I could clearly hear it. We entered a narrow hallway leading to the reception room. The beloved Guardian was standing at the door to greet us. 'Welcome! Welcome! I have been waiting for you,' he said. We tried to cast ourselves at his feet, but he quickly came forward and prevented us, and embracing each of us said, 'We embrace as brothers. The Blessed Beauty has forbidden bowing and prostrating oneself.'*

He asked us to enter the room, and when we had, he entered himself and sat on the divan close to the door, while repeatedly guiding us to take the upper seats. He first asked about the health and conditions of the Bahá'ís and the affairs of the National Spiritual Assembly. When the response was given, he addressed me and said, 'You are the secretary of both the National and Local Spiritual Assemblies. The affairs of the National Spiritual Assembly are conducted in a very organized manner, and I testify to your work. Your services are now local and national, and they will be

* *Á<u>th</u>ár-i-Qalam-i A'lá*, vol. 2, p. 82. And from Maḥmúd's Diary, vol. 2, p. 373: 'Prostration, according to the explicit text of the Book of God, is confined to the Shrine of the Báb, the Shrine of Bahá'u'lláh and the Holy House.'

international in the future.'* He then asked about the persecution of the friends in Iran. I briefly described the difficulties we were facing in obtaining recognition of Bahá'í marriage. He replied that these persecutions were not important and would pass, the principal point being the steadfastness and perseverance of the believers. He then quoted words of 'Abdu'l-Bahá: 'The government of the native land of the Blessed Perfection will become the most respected government of this world . . . and Iran will become the most prosperous of all lands.' (See *Bahá'u'lláh, The King of Glory*, p. 4.) He also emphasized the great importance of Bahá'ís participating in the Nineteen-Day Feasts, then stood up and said, 'You must be very tired. Take leave and rest in the Pilgrim House. I shall see you again tomorrow. May you be in God's protection.'

The meetings of the Persian Bahá'ís with the beloved Guardian usually followed this plan: at 4.00 p.m. every day, the pilgrims of both sexes, in the company of the custodian of the Pilgrim House, would rent a car and drive to the House of 'Abdu'l-Bahá. The ladies then met with Amatu'l-Bahá Rúḥíyyih Kh̲ánum, and the men were guided to the waiting-room. The beloved Guardian would leave his office, join the men and walk with them either in the quiet streets of Haifa or in the gardens of the Shrine of the Báb, speaking with them for about forty minutes or more. He would also accompany the men pilgrims to the Shrines of the Báb and 'Abdu'l-Bahá on two different days, and chant the Tablets of Visitation himself.

While walking with us in the gardens of the Shrine during our second meeting with him, Shoghi Effendi spoke of Muḥammad, Whose station was lofty and great, as the recipient of a Divine Revelation. He returned to this theme on a later occasion, saying that the believers should be

* The reported words of the Guardian, Shoghi Effendi, in the author's recollections of this pilgrimage are not his exact words, which were spoken in Persian and are here summarized. (Editor.)

aware, and believe, that Islam is the origin of the Bahá'í Faith, that the Qur'án is the Word of God and that the Imams were infallible. Their station was very sacred and exalted, particularly that of Imam Ḥusayn (the third Imam, titled the King of Martyrs). As to the traditions of Islam, those which are quoted in the Writings are authentic. He stressed that Bahá'ís of Christian background should accept these principles concerning Islam, just as those of Jewish or Zoroastrian background should accept Christ as the Word of God and His utterances in the New Testament as authentic. The Guardian also wished the friends to realize that each Manifestation can abrogate the laws of previous Manifestations when they no longer meet the needs of the time.

He then spoke of the divines of the University of al-Azhar whose intention was to harm the Faith, while in fact their attacks led to its emancipation in Egypt. Bahá'ís need not fear such events, however ferocious and painful, as they will ultimately and assuredly benefit the Cause. The divines, in fact, announced its independence from Islam, and the Egyptian Government gave the Bahá'ís land for their cemetery. Its cornerstone had recently been laid and the friends had met there. (These events are described in *God Passes By*, chapter 24.)

Because what had happened in Egypt could happen elsewhere, especially in the East, the beloved Guardian emphasized that Bahá'í communities must be distinguished from other communities – he called it days of the 'most great separation' – before the ordained emancipation of the Cause could be realized. The believers must strive that their individual actions, in all aspects of their personal lives, contribute to the emancipation of the Cause. Nor must they conceal their Faith, but cling steadfastly to the Divine laws and teachings. This will attract others, protect the unity of the Bahá'í community, and hasten recognition of the independence of the Faith.

As news of the passing of Hyde Dunn had just reached the Guardian, he spoke of his services, saying that he and his wife were the founders of the Australian Bahá'í community; they recognized him as their spiritual father and called him 'Father Dunn'. (The reader will perhaps know that in 1952 'Mother Dunn' became a Hand of the Cause of God, and, posthumously, 'Father Dunn' was also raised to this station.)

The Second World War in Europe had already begun at the time of our pilgrimage and the Guardian had much in mind what was then happening. One day he talked about the turmoil in the world, referring to the devastating events of the war and the wisdom of calamities sent to heedless humanity to awaken people from their slumber and guide them to the Cause of God. He particularly repeated this warning by Bahá'u'lláh: 'The day is approaching when its [civilization's] flame will devour the cities . . .' (*Gleanings*, CLXIII), and exclaimed, 'Yea! In the flames of an extravagant civilization.' He then explained the need to observe moderation in all things, and reminded us of the utterance of Bahá'u'lláh: 'In all matters moderation is desirable. If a thing is carried to excess, it will prove a source of evil.' (*Tablets of Bahá'u'lláh*, p. 69.) He commented in great detail on the dangers of an extravagant civilization, and of any matter that is carried to excess. Some days later he told us of a letter just received from Manchester, commenting: 'Praise God that the friends of England are all safe in the midst of the devastating events of the war. In such conflicts both sides are defeated. There is no winner or loser. Everybody bears afflictions and harm.'

The turn of events in Bulgaria prompted the beloved Guardian to praise Marion Jack, whom the Master had called 'General Jack', for her services there and for her desire to remain in Bulgaria despite the difficulties she would have in the midst of the war because of her Canadian citizenship.

He asked us to remind the Bahá'í youth and women of Iran to follow her example.

Towards the end of our pilgrimage, Shoghi Effendi again spoke of the women of Iran, who had recently been given relative freedom, the veil (*chadur*) having been abandoned by Government order. He wished the Bahá'í women to take advantage of their freedom and prepare to teach and also engage in various activities. Before long their Western brothers and sisters would come to Iran in troops; they must be welcomed and given hospitality, and the Bahá'í women of Iran must share equally in their services. He urged us to emphasize that they should follow the examples of Martha Root, Mrs Maxwell, Mrs Ransom-Kehler and others like them. And he testified to the fact that Mrs Ransom-Kehler had sacrificed herself for the Bahá'ís of Iran.

Another day he expanded this theme, telling us that in future the Western believers will go to Iran in groups and the Persian friends should be prepared to serve equally with them. They should not allow themselves to remain behind, but deepen in the history of the Faith and the principles of the Administrative Order so that they can serve unitedly with their Western sisters and brothers.

Yet another point expressed by the beloved Guardian for Iran was that the Bahá'ís there should learn Arabic and familiarize themselves with the language of the Writings, so that whether in conversation or in writing, they would express themselves in a similar way. 'The Persian and Arabic languages should dissolve into each other like unto milk and sugar,' he said. Just as the language of the Qur'án was the standard for Islam, so the language of the Writings is now the standard for Bahá'ís.

Early in our pilgrimage we visited, during three days, the Shrine of Bahá'u'lláh, the Qiblih of the people of Bahá, and the Mansion of Bahjí, the House of 'Abbúd, various historical sites in 'Akká, the 'Heaven of Heavens', the Riḍván Garden and Mazra'ih. Because these Holy Places of the Bahá'í Faith as well as some of the other sites have been described in several books published during the last forty years – above all, *God Passes By* by the beloved Guardian, and other sources such as *Bahá'í Holy Places, Bahá'u'lláh, The King of Glory* by Hand of the Cause Hasan Balyuzi, and, most lately, *Door of Hope* by Dr David Ruhe, it is no longer necessary for me to describe many of the things we saw and learned during our pilgrimage, but the following paragraphs will, I hope, be of interest to my readers.

In those days of 1941 pilgrims were privileged to spend two nights in the Mansion of Bahjí, where we visited the room occupied by the Blessed Beauty for over twelve years and in which He ascended. It was here that He received the young English orientalist Edward Granville Browne in the spring of 1890, and I could not but recall his eloquent descriptions of both Bahá'u'lláh and the Master which are justly famous and perhaps already known to the reader, but deserving to be repeated nevertheless.

So here at *Behjé* [sic] was I installed as a guest, in the very midst of all that Bábíism accounts most noble and most holy; and here did I spend five most memorable days, during which I enjoyed unparalleled and unhoped-for opportunities of holding intercourse with those who are the very fountain-heads of that mighty and wondrous spirit which works with invisible but ever-increasing force for the transformation and quickening of a people who slumber in a sleep like unto death. It was in truth a strange and moving experience, but one whereof I despair of conveying any save the feeblest impression. I might, indeed, strive to describe in greater detail the faces and forms which surrounded me, the conversation to which I was privileged to listen, the solemn melodious reading of the sacred books, the general sense of harmony and content which pervaded the place, and the fragrant shady gardens whither in the afternoon we sometimes repaired; but all this was as nought in comparison with the spiritual atmosphere with which I was encompassed . . . The spirit which pervades the Bábís is such that it can hardly fail to affect most powerfully all subjected to its influence. It may appal or attract: it cannot be ignored or disregarded. Let those who have not seen disbelieve me if they will; but, should that spirit once reveal itself to them, they will experience an emotion which they are not likely to forget.

During the morning of the day after my installation at *Behjé* one of Behá's younger sons entered the room where I was sitting and beckoned to me to follow him. I did so, and was conducted through passages and rooms at which I scarcely had time to glance to a spacious hall, paved, so far as I remember (for my mind was occupied with other thoughts) with a mosaic of marble. Before a curtain suspended from the wall of this great ante-chamber my conductor paused for a moment while I removed my shoes. Then, with a quick movement of the hand, he withdrew, and, as I passed, replaced the curtain; and I found myself in a large apartment, along the upper end of which ran a low divan, while on the side opposite to the door were placed two or three chairs. Though I dimly suspected whither I was going and whom I was to behold (for no distinct intimation had been given to me), a second or two elapsed ere, with a throb of wonder and awe, I became definitely conscious that the room was not untenanted. In the corner where the divan met the wall sat a wondrous and venerable figure, crowned with a felt head-dress of the kind called *táj* by dervishes (but of unusual height and make), round the base of which was wound a small white turban. The face of him on whom I gazed I can never forget, though I cannot describe it. Those piercing eyes seemed to read one's very soul; power and authority sat on that ample brow; while the deep lines on the forehead and face implied an age which the jet-black hair and beard flowing down in indistinguishable luxuriance almost to the waist seemed to belie. No need to ask in whose presence I stood, as I bowed myself before one who is the object of a devotion and love which kings might envy and emperors sigh for in vain!

A mild dignified voice bade me be seated, and then continued: 'Praise be to God that thou hast attained! . . . Thou hast come to see a prisoner and an exile . . . We desire but the good of the world and the happiness of the nations; yet they deem us a stirrer up of strife and sedition worthy of bondage and banishment . . . That all nations should become one in faith and all men as brothers; that the bonds of affection and unity between the sons of men should be strengthened; that diversity of religion should cease, and differences of race be annulled – what harm is there in this? . . . Yet so it shall be; these fruitless strifes, these ruinous wars shall pass away, and the "Most Great Peace" shall come . . . Do not you in Europe need this also? Is not this that which Christ foretold? . . . Yet do we see your kings and rulers lavishing their treasures more freely on means for the destruction of the human race than on that which would conduce to the happiness of mankind . . . These strifes and this bloodshed and discord must cease, and all men be as one kindred and one family . . . Let not a man glory in this, that he loves his country; let him rather glory in this, that he loves his kind . . .'

Such, so far as I can recall them, were the words which, besides many others, I heard from Behá. Let those who read them consider well with themselves whether such doctrines merit death and bonds, and whether the world is more likely to gain or lose by their diffusion.

And here is Browne's description of 'Abdu'l-Bahá, then nearly forty-six years of age:

Seldom have I seen one whose appearance impressed me more. A tall strongly-built man holding himself straight as an arrow, with white turban and raiment, long black locks reaching almost to the shoulder, broad powerful forehead indicating a strong intellect combined with an unswerving will, eyes keen as a hawk's, and strongly-marked but pleasing features – such was my first impression of 'Abbás Efendi, 'the master' (*Aḳá*) as he *par excellence* is called by the Bábís. Subsequent conversation with him served only to heighten the respect with which his appearance had from the first inspired me. One more eloquent of speech, more ready of argument, more apt of illustration, more intimately acquainted with the sacred books of the Jews, the Christians, and the Muhammadans, could, I should think, scarcely be found even amongst the eloquent, ready, and subtle race to which he belongs. These qualities, combined with a bearing at once majestic and genial, made me cease to wonder at the influence and esteem which he enjoyed even beyond the circle of his father's followers. About the greatness of this man and his power no one who had seen him could entertain a doubt.

While in Russia I had read the account of Browne's visit to 'Akká in the introduction of the Russian translation of *Kitáb-i-Aqdas* by Captain Alexander Tumanski. Despite his having the assistance of Mírzá Abu'l-Faḍl-i-Gulpáygání and Áqá Mírzá Yúsif-i-Rashtí, Tumanski's translation is very literal and extremely inadequate. When I returned to Iran from my pilgrimage, I read the English version quoted above. (See Balyuzi, *Edward Granville Browne and the Bahá'í Faith*, pp. 50–58, for an account of Browne's journey and these descriptions.)

Our visit to the House of 'Abbúd, now so well known to countless Bahá'í pilgrims, also brought to mind many vivid recollections of the times when the Ancient Beauty had resided there, first in the smaller eastern part which belonged to 'Údí Khammár and later in the larger western part with its balcony overlooking the sea. Bahá'u'lláh had revealed His Book of Laws, *Kitáb-i-Aqdas*, in a room in the eastern part which later He gave to the Master. There I was again reminded of the war in Europe, as I recalled the admonitions of Bahá'u'lláh addressed to the kings in that sacred Book, and remembered particularly His severe warnings to the 'banks of the Rhine' and the 'Spot that art situate on the shores of the two seas' and how the Supreme Manifestation of God in His lonely room, imprisoned within the ancient walls of 'Akká, had foreseen the 'lamentations of Berlin' fifty years later, and the blood-stained shores of the Rhine. (See *Synopsis and Codification of the Laws and Ordinances of the Kitáb-i-Aqdas*, p. 21.)

Later, when we had returned to Haifa, the beloved Guardian spoke to us about the *Kitáb-i-Aqdas*, informing us that future Manifestations of God may abrogate its laws (he had mentioned this earlier when speaking of Muḥammad), but that in this Dispensation 'the laws of God must be carried out with no hesitation, but with justice'. And he quoted these words from the *Kitáb-i-Aqdas*: 'Beware lest ye be indulgent in the Religion of God.' The believers, he said, must not hesitate, fearing that application of the laws might cause sedition or rebellion, or disturb the state of affairs. Should such disturbance occur, they must not be alarmed. (The reader will recall how the Bahá'í schools in Iran were closed by the Government because of obedience to the law respecting Bahá'í Holy Days.) And should any individual Bahá'í intentionally violate the laws of God, he must be warned by the spiritual assembly; if he does not respond, his administrative rights must be removed. But if he sincerely decides to amend his wrongdoing, the past should be forgotten. On a later occasion, he said in a very serious tone that consumption of alcohol is absolutely forbidden in our Faith. He also reminded us that the laws of God are not restricted to the *Kitáb-i-Aqdas*, but that the Pen of Glory subsequently revealed many other Tablets which are designated to supplement the provisions of His Most Holy Book, and he mentioned such Tablets as *Ṭarázát, Tajallíyát, Bis͟hárát* and *Kalimát-i-Firdawsíyyih* (now published by the Universal House of Justice in *Tablets of Bahá'u'lláh* revealed after the *Kitáb-i-Aqdas*).

But to return to our day in 'Akká, I should like to mention some of the historical facts connected with this ancient city. The Master related to pilgrims that 'Acco (Accho, later Acre or 'Akká or 'Akko) was first built by Phoenicians. ('Acco in Phoenician means 'curved triangle'.) Egyptian inscriptions of the fifteenth to thirteenth centuries BC indicate that 'Acco was a part of the ancient Egyptian Empire. It is also mentioned in Judges 1:31.

Afterwards Assyrians and then Persians conquered this area. They were followed by Alexander the Great, the

Seleucids of Syria and the Armenian king, Tigranes the Great, who, one after the other, took over this region until the Roman Empire became its ruler. In AD 636 it was conquered by the Arabs, in 969 by the Fatimid caliphs of Egypt, in 1079 by the Seljuks, and in 1099 by the Crusaders, who ruled Acre (as the Christians called it) with only brief interruption for two centuries. Baldwin I seized Acre in 1104 and it became a part of the Christian Kingdom of Jerusalem. In 1187 Saladin raised the banner of Islam on the towers of Acre, but it was soon recovered for the Christians in the Third Crusade and remained their capital until the Mamluks of Egypt conquered and destroyed the city in 1291.

The construction of the second fortification of Acre was begun in 1202 and completed ten years later. Al-Jazzár fortified the city with a new wall, partly still visible. After the unsuccessful siege of a few months in 1799 by Napoleon I following his invasion of Egypt, al-Jazzár, with support of a British fleet, defeated him. Afterwards the present ramparts were constructed and the sea wall strengthened. Ibrahim Pasha with an Egyptian army took 'Akká in 1832 but in 1840 with the support of British and Austrian naval forces, the fortified city was restored to the Turks. It remained under Ottoman rule until 1917 when it was taken by the British Army. In 1948 the State of Israel was established and 'Akká became one of its historical cities.

There is a well-known tradition concerning 'Akká which states: 'Of all shores the best is the shore of Askelon, and 'Akká is, verily, better than Askelon, and the merit of 'Akká above that of Askelon and all other shores is as the merit of Muḥammad above that of all other Prophets.' (See *Epistle to the Son of the Wolf*, p. 178.)

Ashkelon (Askelon or Ascalon) was an ancient sea-port village on the Mediterranean coast north of Gaza. It was first inhabited about 2000 BC and is mentioned in Egyptian texts of that time. During the next two millenniums the city was under Egyptian, Assyrian, Babylonian and Hellenic rule. Nebuchadnezzar destroyed the city in 604 BC and deported its leading citizens to Babylon, and nearly three centuries later Alexander the Great conquered Ashkelon on his march to Egypt. Afterwards, in AD 636, it was taken by the Arabs. Today, close to the ruins of that old city, is the new city of Migdal-Ashkelon. But of all the ancient and much fought-over cities along the Mediterranean, the Blessed Beauty in many of His Tablets characterized 'Akká as the most ruinous of all. It 'is the most desolate of the cities of the world, the most unsightly of them in appearance . . .' (See *God Passes By*, p. 186.)

During our day in 'Akká we visited the Mosque of al-Jazzár and the Khán-i-'Avámíd, which are both historical places for Bahá'ís, and in imagination travelled back through time witnessing with our inner eyes the dire and woeful events that had occurred there. When the Ancient Beauty and His family were transferred from the barracks to make room for Turkish troops, many of His companions found a home in the Khán-i-'Avámíd. Khán in Turkish means 'inn', and as the inn had pillars ('Avámíd), it became known as the Khán-i-'Avámíd. The inn was built in 1785, and in 1906 a tower was erected at its entrance to commemorate the jubilee of Sultan 'Abdu'l-Ḥamíd. This tower still exists. The Bahá'ís lived mostly in rooms on the top floor of the southern and western wings, and for a time 'Abdu'l-Bahá used and received his guests in one of these rooms.

The Mosque was built by Aḥmad Páshá, known as al-Jazzár. From 1775 to 1804 he was Páshá of 'Akká with authority from Beirut to Caesarea and far eastward, and was known as al-Jazzár (Butcher) because of his notorious cruelty. He had, it is said, ordered the massacre of 70,000 dissidents in Egypt who had rebelled against the Ottoman

Government. (See *al-Munjid fi'l-A'lám.*) He was also the Amíru'l-Ḥajj or leader of the pilgrims to Mecca.

The Master visited this mosque on several occasions, and Badí'-i-Khurásání, who carried the Tablet of Bahá'u'lláh (*Lawḥ-i-Sulṭán*) to the Shah of Iran, first met 'Abdu'l-Bahá there. He then accompanied the Master to the barracks where he twice attained the presence of Bahá'u'lláh.

At the time we were in the Holy Land pilgrimage to the Mansion of Mazra'ih was arranged in the following way. The beloved Guardian, through his secretary, wrote a note to the occupants of Mazra'ih, a retired English officer and his Bahá'í wife, Lilian McNeill. (See *World Order*, vol. 4, p. 10.) We took the note to Mazra'ih, and were subsequently warmly greeted by this family and guided to the room of the Blessed Beauty. Our visit to the barracks, which at the time was a hospital for mental patients, was arranged in a similar way. We took the note written on the Guardian's behalf to the barracks guard, were accompanied by him to the prison cell of the Blessed Beauty and, after finishing our prayers, were escorted back by him.

When we returned to Haifa and attained the presence of the beloved Guardian again, the very first thing he told us was: 'When you return to Iran, the Bahá'ís will come to visit you because it is said in the traditions: "Blessed the man that hath visited 'Akká, and blessed he that hath visited the visitor of 'Akká. Blessed the one that hath drunk from the Spring of the Cow and washed in its waters . . . "' (*Epistle to the Son of the Wolf*, pp. 179–80.) Then he added with a charming smile: 'This tradition also has an addendum: Blessed is he who hath been bitten by the fleas of 'Akká. However, you were deprived of this bounty because there are no longer any fleas in 'Akká. In the past fleas were everywhere in 'Akká.'

He also gave a detailed account of the Mansion of Bahjí, the opposition of the Covenant-breakers, and the efforts that he himself had invested for its repairs and beautification.

We had visited the Spring of the Cow, known as 'Aynu'l-Baqr, during our pilgrimage. It was a cave-like spring with sixteen steps. Stagnant water covered with moss could be seen at the end of the cave, but because it had been mentioned in the traditions of Islam, many people used to travel long distances to see it. On its walls remnants of their offerings of colourful cloths were still hanging from nails. Náṣir Khusraw-i-'Alaví, who visited 'Akká in AH 438, mentioned 'Aynu'l-Baqr in the account of his travels, stating that the inhabitants of that area believed that when Adam was expelled from Paradise, he came to 'Akká and used this spring to water his cow (baqr). Hence its name.

The beloved Guardian spoke to us at several times of the Local and National Spiritual Assemblies and of the Universal House of Justice. These are some of the points he made, according to my recollection.

The National Spiritual Assemblies are very important as they will be the pillars of the Universal House of Justice. Now is the time to strengthen their foundations in both the East and the West. Utmost care should be paid to the election of secretaries for both National and Local Assemblies because their responsibilities and duties are great. It is a matter of conscience for Bahá'ís to participate in Bahá'í elections and neglect of this spiritual duty is a serious matter. With regard to consultation, the Master has said that first we must consult, then deliberate, then reach a decision, and finally carry out that decision. Consultation without result, the Guardian concluded, is futile. The Universal House of Justice, although not the National and Local Assemblies, is infallible, but the individuals are not, an important point requiring our utmost attention. Infallibility is solely the characteristic of the Universal House of Justice.

The beloved Guardian also mentioned that Assemblies

and all other Bahá'í institutions should demonstrate justice and equity in all matters, since justice is the foundation of society. The Blessed Beauty ordained the 'House of Justice', not the 'House of Forgiveness' or the 'House of Grace'. The foundation of the world and the realization of the Most Great Peace are dependent upon justice. Without justice there will be no peace, and disorder and confusion will prevail. Once again the Guardian stressed that believers who transgress against the Teachings should be punished by the Assemblies if and when their warning, admonitions and advice are not heeded, and they should have no hesitation in doing so, particularly if the transgressor is one of the well-known Bahá'ís. When the believers see that the Assemblies treat every one equally, high and low alike, they will be encouraged and will follow their example. However, when individuals express their regret and repent, the past should be dismissed.

Expanding his discussion of these institutions of the Faith, the Guardian explained that the Religion of God rests on two pillars: laws and principles. The principles are of two kinds, spiritual and administrative. The first are fully expounded in the writings and talks of the Master, and the second are defined in the Declaration of Trust and By-Laws. One cannot compare the Administrative Order of Bahá'u'lláh with any other system, for it is a totally new Order and has no precedent in past history. (See *The World Order of Bahá'u'lláh*, pp. 152–4.) The Administrative Order is the prelude to World Order, which in turn is the prelude to a Divine Civilization: the fruit of the tree of the Cause of God.

We were given a wonderful vision of the future by the beloved Guardian. The last stage in achieving the maturity of the world will be the unity of mankind. At this time we cannot comprehend the glory of the Revelation of Bahá'u'lláh. Although another Manifestation of God may appear after a thousand years, for 500,000 years all the Manifestations will be under the shadow of the Blessed Beauty. Then the Guardian quoted words of the Master, 'that in so far as their relation to the source of their inspiration is concerned they are under the shadow of the Ancient Beauty. In their relation, however, to the age in which they appear, each and every one of them "doeth whatsoever He willeth".' (*God Passes By*, p. 99.)

On the ninth day of our pilgrimage, Monday, 24 February, we went to the House of the Master to meet the beloved Guardian. Upon our arrival he left his study and joined us. A rented car was waiting, and the Guardian told us that he himself would accompany us for an outing. We went outside and he took a seat in the back of the car, asking the other pilgrims to take the other seats. On his invitation I sat by him, and in observing due respect tried to maintain my distance and pressed my right arm against the car. He instructed the driver to go towards Mount Carmel, but as the car drove up the slope of the mountain I lost control and my shoulder and knee touched the beloved Guardian. I was greatly disturbed, and even though it was cold outside, a cold sweat covered my forehead. He kindly comforted me, saying, 'Be quiet, be calm.'

On the way the beloved Guardian talked in detail about the history of Haifa, the wars of the Crusaders, and other historical events of Palestine. When we reached the top of Mount Carmel, close to the present site of the future Mashriqu'l-Adhkár, the car stopped. He left the car and we followed him. And then, facing the Shrine of Bahá'u'lláh, he said: 'The Master has repeatedly said that the view of Haifa from Mount Carmel is one of the best in the world because it includes sea, mountain and plain together.' He then added, 'The first Bahá'í Mashriqu'l-Adhkár was built on the plain of 'Ishqábád. The second Mashriqu'l-Adhkár was built on the banks of Lake Michigan. The Mashriqu'l-Adhkár of Tehran will be built on the slope of a mountain. When the Mashriqu'l-Adhkár of Haifa is erected on Mount Carmel, its view will include all the three views: sea, mountain and plain.' A few minutes later we went back to the car and drove to the House of the Master. There he dismissed us by saying, 'May you be under the protection of God', and we took the same car to the Pilgrim House with our hearts filled with joy and gratitude for having had such a great bounty and privilege.

The next day the beloved Guardian again walked with the pilgrims in the gardens of the Shrine of the Báb, speaking of the events which led to the building of the Shrine. He told us that the Prophet Isaiah had prophesied that on the Last Day the Tabernacle of the Lord would be pitched on the Mountain of God. This prophecy was fulfilled when Bahá'u'lláh pitched His tent on Mount Carmel. It was then that He indicated to 'Abdu'l-Bahá the land which should be purchased for the interment of the remains of the Báb. Therefore, the choice of this location was not by chance. The Bahá'ís should note that Bahá'u'lláh Himself was the Founder of the Shrine, and the Master was the executor of His plan. The purchase of the properties around the Shrine of the Báb were made possible by the sacrifices of the Bahá'ís of Iran.

The Guardian also commented on certain features of the Shrine, speaking first of the terraces, nine below the Shrine already developed, and in the future nine additional terraces from the Shrine to the top of the mountain. Each terrace will be illumined by electricity; it will be 'light upon light', he said. He also spoke of the Master's plan that the Shrine should have nine rooms; six of these He Himself built and after His ascension three were added. The Master named the five doors of the original Shrine rooms after several believers: Báb-i-Amín, Báb-i-Faḍl, Báb-i-Ashraf, Báb-i-

Bálá, and Báb-i-Karím. (The Hand of the Cause Dr Giachery has fully explained the naming of these doors in his book entitled *Shoghi Effendi, Recollections*, Appendix 9.)

Towards the end of our pilgrimage the beloved Guardian commented on various points concerning individual Bahá'ís. Having explained the qualifications for members of the Faith, he said that everyone should be accorded absolute freedom to choose whether to join the Bahá'í community or not. However, since Bahá'ís should not participate in politics even in conversation, it is very important not to accept into the Faith under any circumstances those who do participate in politics.

He then spoke of pioneering and described the three important qualifications of a pioneer: to arise transported by divine love, to trust wholly in the Blessed Beauty, and to demonstrate absolute perseverance. Bahá'ís should prepare themselves for pioneering and keep these qualifications in mind. They should also realize that the purpose of pioneering is not trade and commerce, but to serve the Cause. He urged Bahá'í youth to deepen themselves in the history, laws and principles of the Faith as preparation for teaching both in Iran and neighbouring countries. Perseverance, he told us, in itself is the remover of all obstacles.

Other instructions of the Guardian for individual Bahá'ís concerned contributing to charitable institutions that benefit mankind, preferably through their National Assembly, but in their own names if this is not accepted. Such contributions should not be given as a gesture, but with the intention of being helpful. And finally, Bahá'ís should shun Covenant-breakers, at the same time considering it a duty to try to remove the doubts that may be present in the minds of fellow believers.

There were various interesting comments made by the beloved Guardian, usually without elaboration, that I should like to share. He had just received a letter from

London stating that Christophil (a pseudonym used by George Townshend for the first publication of *The Promise of All Ages*) was writing a response to a book written by a Protestant priest against the Faith. Opposition by opponents of the Faith will be intensified in the future in both the East and West, he said, and the Bahá'ís should write full and adequate replies.

He told us, also, about Monsieur Nicolas, the French orientalist, who greatly admired the Báb but imagined that the Bahá'ís undervalued His station. Hearing that he was very disturbed about this, the Guardian sent him a copy of *The Dawn-Breakers*. He expressed his gratitude and his admiration of the book.

At another time the beloved Guardian explained certain points in the Writings. The title of the *Súriy-i-Haykal* ('Haykal' meaning body or temple) refers to the style adopted for a few of Bahá'u'lláh's Tablets which were written on His instructions in a very small handwriting in the form of a human temple. Tablets addressed to the Tsar of Russia, Napoleon III, Queen Victoria and the Shah of Persia were written in this style. He added that the Báb also addressed the kings and rulers of the world. The term 'Ghuṣn' (Branch) refers not only to 'Abdu'l-Bahá but in one sense to the person of the Ancient Beauty, and the Master has confirmed this in *Some Answered Questions*. In this Dispensation, he also told us, 'Holy Book' is changed to 'Most Holy Book', and 'Holy Spirit' to 'Most Holy Spirit'. Therefore, the 'Greatest Name', the 'Most Great Peace', and the 'Most Great Dispensation'. An important point was made by the Guardian concerning Nabíl's Narrative (*The Dawn-Breakers*), which he said is authentic and the accurate source of the early history of the Faith. Bahá'í historians should verify their findings in this book.

Although at the time of our pilgrimage in 1941 its duration was normally nineteen days, the beloved Guardian extended our time to twenty-three days. This was because the railroad connecting Palestine to Syria had been damaged by heavy rains and we would have to await its repair. The day before my departure the beloved Guardian instructed me to return to Iran via Damascus, spend a few days there with the friends, and remind them on his behalf to proceed with acquiring their Ḥaẓíratu'l-Quds. He then cabled them about my visit.

So came the last day of our pilgrimage, Monday, 10 March. All the pilgrims, both men and women, gathered together in the guest room of the House of the Master to meet the beloved Guardian for the last time. He came in truly as radiant as a full moon, and we stood up in respect. He asked us to take our seats. On a table in front of his seat there were a few books, pictures, and various papers. He admonished us once again to demonstrate utmost patience and perseverance in facing the difficulties and afflictions in the path of God, and at the end of his talk instructed us to convey his greetings to the friends of Iran. He then gave me a copy of the Arabic version of Nabíl's Narrative (*The Dawn-Breakers*), which was newly translated by 'Abdu'l-Jalíl Bey Sa'ad in Egypt, to present to the National Spiritual Assembly of Iran. Then he bade us farewell, and we, with much sorrow, left his blessed presence.

6

From Haifa to Tehran

Our family took the train on the same night and arrived in Damascus at 11.30 p.m. A group of Bahá'ís had come to greet us at the station. We stayed in Damascus a few days and were able to convey the instructions of the beloved Guardian to the friends. The city enjoys a pleasant climate and is surrounded by numerous orchards. Crystal-clear running water is provided for many homes.

I have an interesting memory from this trip when my mother, my wife, our daughter and I were occupying one of the compartments on the train, two seats being vacant. We had just left Haifa when a young Arab asked permission to enter and sit with us. He was well dressed and very courteous and dignified. After a few moments a conversation began, and he asked our names and destination. I told him that we were Bahá'ís and were on our way to Damascus after our visit to Haifa. His face was suddenly illumined and he said: 'Blessed are you. His Holiness 'Abbás Effendi was a kind father to all of us.' He then told us that he was a Christian and a native of Haifa and had heard many stories from his parents about how 'Abdu'l-Bahá fathered the poor, and how he bore innumerable difficulties to save people from hunger and disease. He also said that the Master had given a prayer-rug to his family, on which they would say their prayers whenever they had a wish. Then as his destination was approaching, he called his mother from the next compartment and introduced my family to her. When she heard that we had just left the House of the Master, she embraced my mother and wife and showered them with affection. They left us with tears in their eyes, as though parting with members of their own family.

On Friday, 14 March, we left Damascus and arrived in Baghdad the next day. We spent one week in the 'City of God' and met the friends on numerous occasions to share news of the Holy Land with them. We also visited Ctesiphon, about twenty miles from Baghdad, where the grave of Salmán the Pure (the first Persian follower of Muḥammad) lies, beside the now-ruined palace of the Sásánian kings. Also buried there is Ḥájí Mírzá Muḥammad-'Alí, the Afnán, whom 'Abdu'l-Bahá praised in *Memorials of the Faithful* (pp. 16–21), saying that 'a magnificent Mashriqu'l-Adhkár must be raised' at his burial site. Here, where this 'throne city of Persia's ancient kings' once stood, we recalled this verse by Kháqání:

> Behold! O thou who gazeth upon
> the wonders of the world,
> Behold with thine inner eyes,
> And learn a lesson
> From Ayván-i-Madá'in.

And words from 'Umar-i-Khayyám also came to mind:

> The Palace that to Heav'n his pillars threw,
> And Kings the forehead on his threshold drew –
> I saw the solitary kingdove there,
> And 'coo, coo, coo', she cried and 'coo, coo, coo'.

And then we thought of the Master's promise that another 'proud city will rise up on this site'. Please God that future generations may witness that glorious day!

On Sunday, 23 March, we left Baghdad for Khániqayn. On the border our luggage was carefully inspected, and we entered Qasr-i-Shirin. We stayed over night, and on the following day left for Kermanshah, where we remained a week to visit the friends. We continued our journey to

Hamadán, and again met the friends for six days to convey news of the Holy Land. While there we visited the burial place of Ibn-i-Síná (Avicenna) and the tombs which tradition assigns to Esther and Mordecai. Qazvin was our next stop, where we arrived on the evening of Sunday, 6 April. For four days, in this birthplace of Ṭáhirih, we were with the friends, and visited the city's historical sites and mosques.

Our month-long journey brought us at last to Tehran on 11 April. Numerous meetings were held with the friends to share the glad-tidings of the Holy Land. Of course, whether in these meetings or those in the cities where we had stopped, our talks were introduced with the reminder that they summarized only what the beloved Guardian had told us in his talks and instructions, and that his messages stemmed from, and were all recorded in, the sacred Writings or his own letters. We also quoted this utterance of the Master: 'Thou hast written concerning the pilgrims and pilgrims' notes. Any narrative that is not authenticated by a Text should not be trusted. Narratives, even if true, cause confusion . . . the Text, and only the Text, is authentic.' (From a Tablet to the Hand of the Cause Ibn-i-Aṣdaq.)

A report of our journey was sent to the beloved Guardian and the following is, in part, his reply (through his secretary):

12 Jamál 98 [20 April 1941]

He instructed me to write that your visit and companionship with you in the vicinity of the illumined Holy Shrines were a cause of exceeding joy. There is no doubt that after this pilgrimage and your prayers for aid and grace at the sacred Threshold of the Abhá Beauty – the Point round which the Concourse on high revolve – and the Shrines of the Báb, and of 'Abdu'l-Bahá, you will be privileged to render greater . . . services.

In 1944, the hundredth anniversary of the Declaration of

the Báb was joyously and befittingly celebrated by all the Bahá'í communities in Iran. The National Convention of that blessed year was held in the illumined city of Shíráz. On several occasions the Convention delegates visited the Holy House of the Báb and the beloved Guardian's message dated Naw-Rúz, BE 101, was read in its vicinity. Numerous meetings were held, attended in great numbers by the Bahá'ís of Shíráz and neighbouring towns.

During the same year three believers, Muḥammad-i-Jadhbání, Asadu'lláh Nádirí, and Muhájir Anárakí, were martyred in Shahrúd. Their tragic deaths released a new spiritual energy, rekindling in the hearts of the believers of Iran their devotion and love of God.

Two years later the Iranian Radio and Broadcasting Service invited me to give a series of lectures on children's education. This programme was continued once a week for six months, became nationally known, and I received many commendations from various non-Bahá'ís. In later years the text of these lectures, together with other articles, was published with the permission of the Ministry of Education in a book entitled *Essays on Education* (Maghálát-i-Tarbíyatí), which was repeatedly reprinted. Much later the substance of these talks and essays was published in English as *Mothers, Fathers and Children* (George Ronald, 1980).

In 1950, according to the instructions of the beloved Guardian, the hundredth anniversary of the Martyrdom of the Báb was commemorated. The Bahá'ís of Iran joined their sisters and brothers throughout the world in mourning the martyrdom of their Beloved, and recalled the sufferings that were endured by Him and many of His followers in the Heroic Age of the Faith. The *Bahá'í News* of Iran published a special issue for this occasion, to which I contributed an article. It was later translated into English and reprinted in India on several occasions.

First Contingent of Hands of the Cause of God

The month of December 1951 marks a momentous transformation in my spiritual life. In this month I received the cable of the beloved Guardian appointing me a Hand of the Cause of God. At the same time I heard that Jináb-i-Valíyu'lláh Varqá and Jináb-i-Ṭaráẓu'lláh Samandarí had also been elevated to this rank. I have never been able to offer enough gratitude at the Holy Threshold for bestowing on me such an honour. Later, we received the message of the beloved Guardian appointing, on the same date, nine other Bahá'ís in the Holy Land, Europe and America, bringing to twelve the number of this first contingent of Hands of the Cause of God. Seven others were appointed in February 1952, raising their number to a Váḥid (nineteen).

During the same year, 1952, we received a message from the beloved Guardian addressed to the believers of Iran, encouraging contributions for the construction of the superstructure of the Shrine of the Báb. The National Spiritual Assembly of Iran, in co-operation with the Local Spiritual Assembly of Tehran and its committees, invited the Bahá'ís of Tehran to attend thirteen consecutive meetings held for this purpose. Although it was a severely cold winter and heavy snow was on the ground, the believers in utmost joy and ecstasy came, usually from long distances and on foot, to attend these meetings in the Ḥaẓíratu'l-Quds. Throughout these thirteen nights, the jubilant meetings always began with prayers, then the letter of the beloved Guardian on the significance of the construction of the superstructure of the Shrine of the Báb was read, and after that the friends offered their contributions. They included everything from cash to valuable gifts, so spontaneously offered that soon afterwards the Guardian cabled that no more contributions were needed. He later told pilgrims that the Bahá'ís of Iran had undertaken the lion's share of contributions, and that it was enough!

7

World Travels in the First Year of the Ten Year Crusade

When the detailed plans for the Ten Year Crusade were announced in 1953 the duties and responsibilities of the Hands of the Cause were increased, and the beloved Guardian guided and encouraged them to participate in the Bahá'í Intercontinental Teaching Conferences that were to be held in the continents of Africa, America, Europe and Asia. My year-long journey began at this time.

It was in the company of twenty-six other believers from Tehran, at noon on 26 January 1953, that we set out for Baghdad, arriving there some two hours later. A group of Bahá'ís greeted us at the airport. The same afternoon we attended two meetings, first with the Bahá'í women and then with the Bahá'í men, in the beautiful Ḥaẓíratu'l-Quds of that illumined city. We gave them a message of love on behalf of the Iranian friends and later visited the Library and National Archives of the Bahá'ís of Iraq.

Our next stop was Cairo, where a meeting was held in the Ḥaẓíratu'l-Quds for the Bahá'ís of both sexes, in the three languages of Arabic, Persian, and English. We also visited the graves of Mírzá Abu'l-Faḍl, Lua Getsinger (they were adjacent to each other), Áqá Muḥammad Taqíy-i-Iṣfahání, and Mr Gulistánih in the Bahá'í cemetery. Here we recited prayers and asked the assistance of these sanctified souls in serving the Holy Threshold. While in Cairo we saw the famous Islamic University of al-Azhar and the Shrine of Rasu'l-Ḥusayn, located in one of the best areas of the city. This Shrine was very beautiful, yet simple and serene. 'Abdu'l-Bahá had mentioned it several times in His talks.

Kampala and Europe

We then left for Kampala, capital of Uganda, where the African Intercontinental Teaching Conference was to be held, and after twelve hours of travel landed at its airport. A few of the friends had come to greet us and bring us to the city.

Kampala is very beautiful, situated on hills with many shrubs and flowers of various colours. On 12 February 1953, eighty black believers and a great number of Persian, American, English, Egyptian and other Bahá'ís had gathered together for the first session of the Conference, under a large tent raised on the grounds of the Ḥaẓíratu'l-Quds. Before the close of the Conference on 18 February, some 232 Bahá'ís from 19 countries had gathered, the African believers from 18 tribes of Uganda and North Africa constituting the majority of those attending.

The Conference was opened with prayers read in different languages, followed by the Guardian's Message, presented by his representative, Hand of the Cause Leroy Ioas. The joy of the beloved Guardian at the attendance of such an 'unexpectedly large number of the representatives of the pure-hearted and the spiritually receptive Negro race', and their 'preponderance . . . at so significant a Conference, a phenomenon unprecedented in the annals of Bahá'í Conferences held during a century', exhilarated the friends and inspired the African Bahá'ís to take their full share in the consultations. Among the several talks on the significance of the occasion, the words of a new African believer were memorable: 'Many . . . have come to this country and have preached their beliefs for years, but not one of them has succeeded in eliminating our racial, religious, and tribal prejudices and uniting us together. We testify with our hearts and spirits that Bahá'u'lláh is the second coming of Christ, and the unity of mankind will be established under the banner of the Bahá'í Faith.'

Dr Richard St Barbe Baker, known as the 'Man of the Trees', who was instrumental in planting thousands of trees in barren areas of Africa and who was related to one of the explorers of that continent, spoke on the exalted station and universality of the teachings of Bahá'u'lláh, deeply moving the friends.

The Hands of the Cause of God and other speakers also contributed to the glory and spirit of the Conference, among whom Hand of the Cause Músá Banání rendered great services and Hand of the Cause Dorothy Baker inspired the friends in her inimitable manner. One of the most unforgettable and historical events of the Conference was the unveiling of the portrait of the Báb, which had been placed on a table covered with a gold-woven cloth adorned with baskets of flowers. Two Hands of the Cause stood at either end of the table, and the believers, deep in meditation and prayer, reverently and silently walked past the portrait, expressing their devotion in their own ways. This spiritual march continued for some time, the faces of the friends reflecting their inner peace and spiritual tranquillity. I recalled the utterance of the Báb to Dr Cormick in Tabríz, when He told the English physician that He had no doubt that all Europeans would come to His Faith. (Balyuzi, *The Báb*, p. 146.) At that time, the reality of this utterance was beyond reach, but in the conference we witnessed the dawn of the fulfilment of His promise at this early stage of His Revelation.

After the conclusion of the Intercontinental Conference, a number of the Hands of the Cause, including myself, and a group of Bahá'ís decided to go on to Europe. We went first to Italy, and in Rome in the course of a few meetings met the beloved friends and conveyed to them the glad-tidings and news of the Kampala Conference. One gathering during the Ayyám-i-Há, when the friends in Rome were preparing themselves for the period of the Fast, was particularly spirited and added much to our joy. Another special occasion was when the Hand of the Cause Dorothy Baker invited Bahá'ís of Rome and a number of other friends from different countries to break their fast in her hotel. The radiance, spirituality, sincerity, and love that animated those who were present in that gathering, who had embraced the Faith each from a different background, and who were together enjoying each other as members of one family, is truly beyond any description.

Several of the Hands of the Cause and I left Italy for Switzerland and met the Bahá'ís in Geneva and Bern. In the meeting in Geneva, attended by both Bahá'ís and seekers, I spoke of the transforming power of the Faith. My talk was translated into French and at the end of the meeting a Swiss scholar, well-known as author and lecturer, expressed his admiration for the Bahá'í teachings and his joy that the Master had blessed Geneva with His footsteps.

Also, in one of the meetings arranged in Geneva, a few of the pilgrims who had just come from the Holy Land were present and one of them, an American believer, conveyed the greetings of the beloved Guardian to all the participants, which added much to the spirit of the occasion.

On 5 March I and the Hand of the Cause Mr 'Alá'í visited the resting-place of Malíḥih Khánum Dhabíḥ, one of the Persian pioneers who had passed away at her pioneering post, and recited a few prayers in memory of the services of that maidservant of God. We also visited Montreux where Dagmar Dole, another steadfast pioneer, is buried. She was much favoured and loved by the Guardian, and after her passing he sent Miss Edna True, chairman of the European Teaching Committee and daughter of the Hand of the

The African Intercontinental Teaching Conference, Kampala, Uganda, 12–18 February 1953

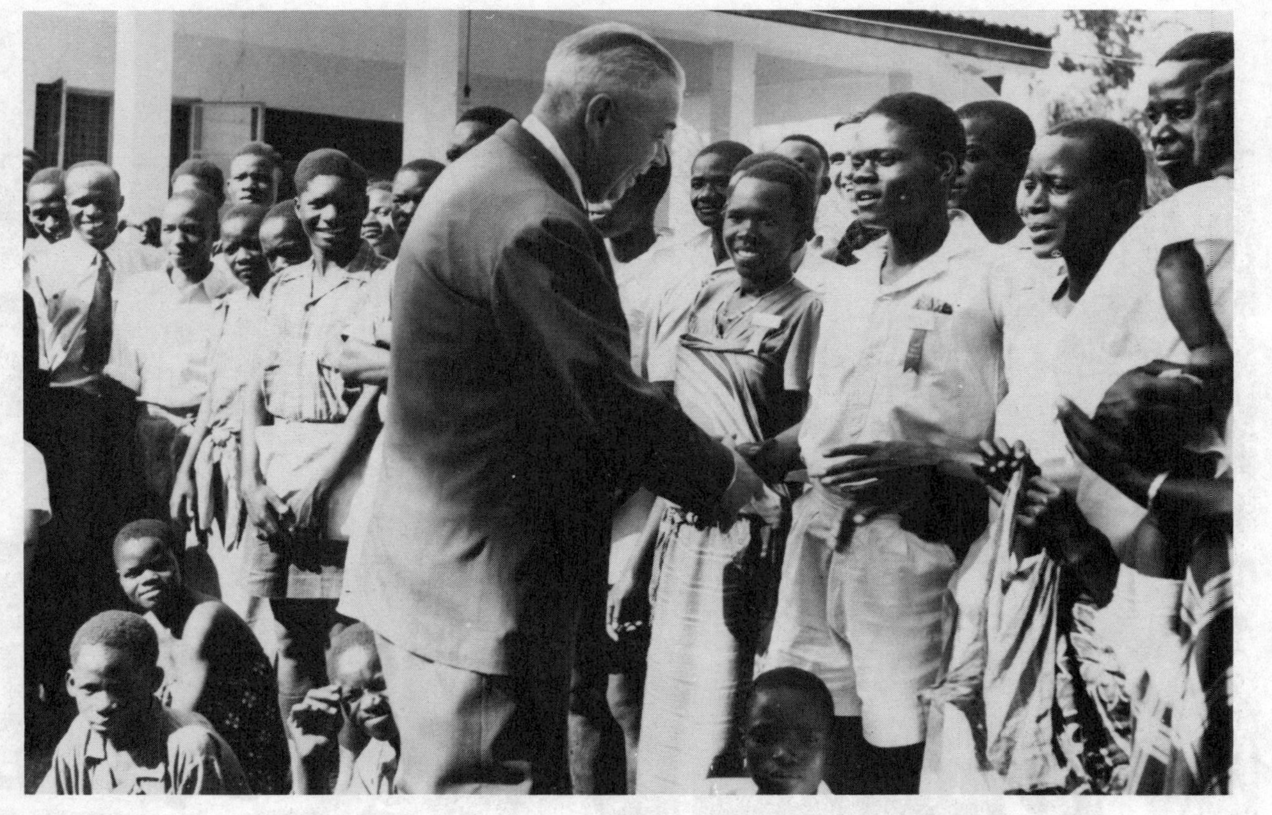

The Hand of the Cause Leroy Ioas, the representative of the Guardian, greeting the African delegates in Kampala, 1953

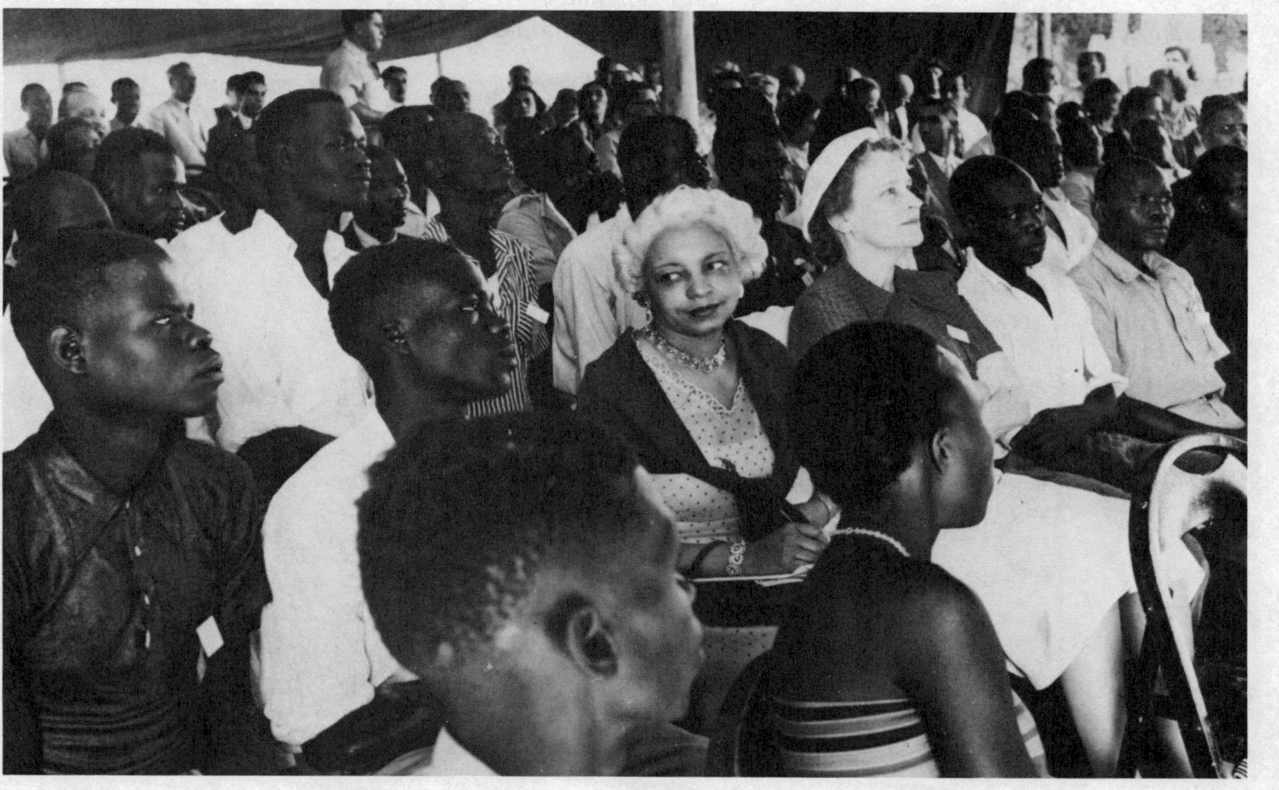

The Intercontinental Teaching Conference in session, Kampala, 1953

Bahá'í pioneers in Africa attending the Intercontinental Teaching Conference, Kampala, 1953

Cause Mrs Corinne True, to participate in her funeral service. Her grave is located on a hill above Montreux, and after we had said a few prayers we left two small silver vases on her grave in memory of this visit.

We then visited the friends of Bern, the capital of Switzerland, and after sharing our news departed for Holland. Innumerable meetings for Bahá'ís and seekers were held in Amsterdam and other places where Bahá'ís were living. We also visited many historical places, museums and churches, and at the end of March 1953 concluded our weeks in Europe and began preparations for our tour of North America.

New York, New Jersey and Ohio

In April 1953 we left by air for the United States and after a few hours were greeted at the airport in New York by several of the Bahá'í friends. Thus began our tour of the United States and Canada. We spent a few days in New York, which the Master has designated the 'City of the Covenant', meeting with the friends. I also visited the Bahá'ís in Englewood and other places in New Jersey, and since there was time before the Intercontinental Teaching Conference to be held in Chicago, in the company of two other friends I left for Akron, Ohio, one of the industrial cities of America. After meeting the Bahá'ís and many seekers, I left for Cleveland, which was honoured with the footsteps of the Master. A few elderly Bahá'ís, who had been privileged to meet 'Abdu'l-Bahá, lived in this city and we called on them, also meeting other believers, after which I returned to New York.

In New York I decided to go and see the Statue of Liberty, which is truly an outstanding work of art. Its sculptor was Frédéric Auguste Bartholdi, a famous artist of the late nineteenth century. Although of Italian descent, he was born in France and lived in that country. The original value of the statue was estimated at $250,000, which in 1884 was a considerable amount. Its construction took two years, and 120 tons of steel and 8 tons of copper were used. Seventy railroad cars were needed to carry the material, and three months were spent to assemble it. On 17 June 1885 the statue was taken by ship to New York, escorted by other ships, where seventy-five men worked for six months to erect its hundred pieces on the foundation, using 300,000 rivets. Finally, in mid-October 1886, the torch of liberty was installed. The President of the United States, Grover Cleveland, unveiled the statue on 28 October 1886, describing it as a symbol of the friendship and respect felt by the people of France for the United States. Mr Bartholdi, who received the Legion of Honour, died on 4 October 1904 in Paris.

The All-America Intercontinental Teaching Conference

From New York I travelled to Chicago to attend the second Intercontinental Teaching Conference, 3 through 6 May 1953, held in one of the famous conference halls of that city. Over 2,300 Bahá'ís from thirty-three countries attended this historic event, and Amatu'l-Bahá Rúḥíyyih Khánum represented the beloved Guardian. Eleven other Hands of the Cause were present, including all five of the Persian Hands. The Conference was opened with prayers and the message of the Guardian, and then consultation began on the goals of the Ten Year Crusade. Since a detailed account of the proceedings of this Conference is published in *The Bahá'í World* (vol. XII, pp. 133–67), only a brief review will be given here. Most of the talks concerned pioneering, and it was my privilege to describe how the Bahá'í youth of Iran were prepared for pioneering, the two aspects of personal preparation through prayer and study, and administrative co-operation with assemblies and committees being stressed. On the day the volunteers were asked to introduce themselves, one hundred and twenty-eight (twenty-two being added later) came on to the stage and most announced their preferred pioneering posts. It is impossible to describe the spirit of that occasion. The audience was so moved that some friends wept for joy.

The historic days when Amatu'l-Bahá Rúḥíyyih Khánum, the Hands of the Cause of God and other Bahá'ís gathered to dedicate the Mother-Temple of the West are truly unforgettable. As the auditorium of the House of Worship could not accommodate all the believers and public at one time, three ceremonies were held. More than 4,000 people comprised those illumined congregations. The first, on 1 May, was for Bahá'ís only, but on 2 May, the Public Dedication took place in the presence of eleven hundred persons. The programme was as follows:

1. Songs by the Bahá'í choir
2. The Message of the Guardian of the Cause of God, read by his representative, Amatu'l-Bahá Rúḥíyyih Khánum
3. Reading of verses from the Old Testament
4. Reading of verses from the New Testament
5. Reading of verses from the Qur'án
6. Songs by the Bahá'í choir
7. Excerpts from the Writings of the Báb in Arabic
8. Excerpts in English from the Commentary of the Báb on the *Súriy-i-Joseph*
9. Excerpts from the Writings of the Báb in Persian
10. Excerpts from the Writings in English
11. Excerpts from the *Epistle to the Son of the Wolf* in English
12. Prayer in English
13. Prayer in Persian
14. Songs by the Bahá'í choir

The third day, 3 May, was again for Bahá'ís only, and it was held, like the other two days, with glory and majesty in the auditorium of the House of Worship. Amatu'l-Bahá Rúḥíyyih Khánum stood by the entrance door inside the Temple and anointed the believers with attar of rose, blessed in the Holy Shrines. After all had taken their seats, she unveiled the portraits of the Báb and the Abhá Beauty, and the believers silently passed by them. Included in the programme was the recitation of the 'Rashḥ-i-'Amá' and other prayers, and the session was then concluded in utmost unity and order.

The present author must confess his inability to convey adequately to readers the beauty and grandeur of those three gatherings. One would have had to be present in such meetings to see for himself. As the poet says:

Thou sayest 'Joseph',
 and thou hast heard of his beauty,
But what worlds of difference
 between hearing and seeing!

Across Canada

After the conclusion of the Conference, a cable was received from the beloved Guardian addressed to the Hands of the Cause of God, directing the Persian Hands to travel in North, Central and South America in the interim period between this and the next Intercontinental Conference in Europe to be held in Stockholm in July 1953. Therefore, I went to Canada and, on the recommendation of the National Spiritual Assembly of the Bahá'ís of Canada, I visited Winnipeg, Saskatoon, Edmonton, Vancouver, Victoria, Calgary, Regina, Hamilton, London (Ontario), St Catharines, Toronto, Ottawa, Belleville, Kingston, Montreal, St Lambert, Verdun, Westmount, the Summer School at Beaulac, Moncton, Charlottetown, Halifax, and St John. These included twenty-one of Canada's thirty Local Spiritual Assemblies. In all these visits, I met with the Bahá'ís and discussed the Faith with seekers in fireside

The grave of Dagmar Dole, Bahá'í pioneer to Alaska, Denmark and Italy, who died 12 November 1952 and is buried at Glion, near Montreux, Switzerland.

The All-America Intercontinental Teaching Conference, Chicago, 3–6 May 1953

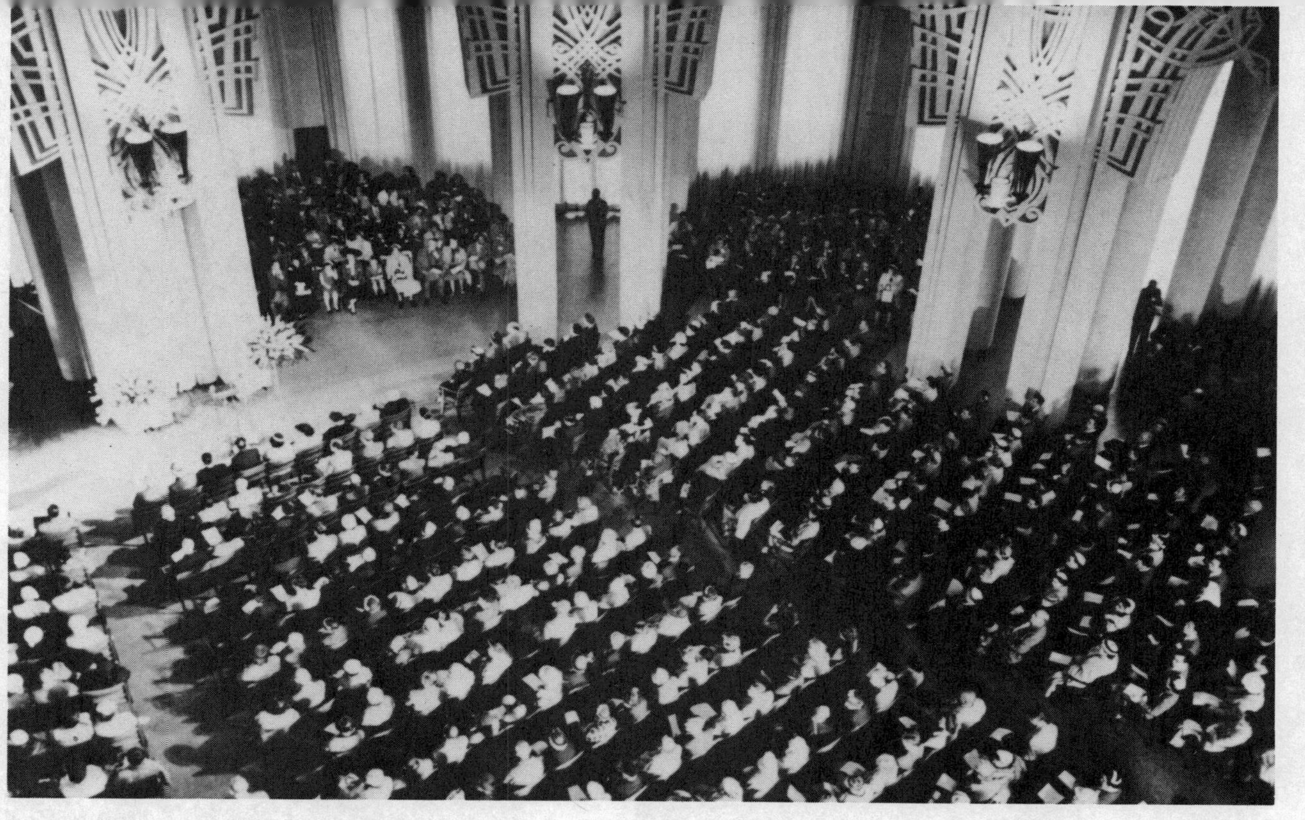

One of three services held to dedicate the Mother-Temple of the West, Wilmette, Illinois, 1–3 May 1953

The Hand of the Cause Amatu'l-Bahá Rúḥíyyih Khánum, the representative of the Guardian, meeting Bahá'ís at the dedication of the Mashriqu'l-Adhkár in Wilmette, May 1953

meetings. I also met with a number of newspaper owners, a minister of education and other scholars, a Kiwanis Club, and spoke on radio, explaining to all the principles of the Bahá'í teachings. Reports of these interviews and talks were later published in many newspapers and magazines. For the Canadian believers it was, they have written, the first opportunity for most of them to meet a Bahá'í from the birthplace of the Faith. They were thrilled to hear at first hand of conditions in Iran and to realize, from my explanations of the teachings and the satisfactory solutions which I offered for the individual problems of some of the friends, 'the universality of the Faith and its ability to solve the problems of the world'.

My travels in Canada continued for 48 days, and I have many sweet memories from that trip, of which I would like to recount a few:

1. When I was on my way to Hamilton from St Catharines, I passed through the border city of the United States and Canada which is located in the vicinity of Niagara Falls. As there were no Bahá'ís there, my companion who was a very devoted Bahá'í suggested that we could either visit the Falls or continue our journey. Because I expressed my deep desire to see that masterpiece of nature we purchased tickets, and after putting on protective leather clothing, boots, and dark glasses, descended to the bottom of the valley where the water of two rivers majestically and forcefully falls, and took our place in the designated tourist area. At this point my companion suggested that we read to ourselves the Tablet of Aḥmad, as the sound of the water prevented us from hearing each other, adding that since, perhaps, no one had ever read the Tablet there, this would be our privilege and we could also make a wish that a Spiritual Assembly be established in that town. We did so, and after a while left, returned the clothing, and went to a restaurant that overlooked the Falls. There she again asked

me if I had recalled any particular excerpts from the Writings while watching the Falls. I said that I hadn't, but she had recalled these words of Bahá'u'lláh in *Epistle to the Son of the Wolf*: 'During the days I lay in the prison of Ṭihrán, though the galling weight of the chains and the stench-filled air allowed Me but little sleep, still in those infrequent moments of slumber I felt as if something flowed from the crown of my head over my breast, *even as a mighty torrent that precipitateth itself upon the earth from the summit of a lofty mountain* . . .' (p. 22, italics added). She recited this passage from memory, and I was greatly astonished at her sharp memory and delicate imagination. A few years later in Haifa, when I was awaiting the arrival of the pilgrims by the Pilgrim House, I saw this same believer among them. She immediately recognized me and said: 'Do you remember that we recited the Tablet of Aḥmad at Niagara Falls, wishing that a Spiritual Assembly be formed there? Well, now there are ten believers and we have indeed formed an Assembly!'

2. In Montreal, accompanied by several Bahá'ís, I visited the Maxwell home, which is a shrine for the Canadian Bahá'í community. 'Abdu'l-Bahá had stayed there in 1912, and many Bahá'ís had received its hospitality. We then visited the resting-place of Hand of the Cause Sutherland Maxwell, the father of Amatu'l-Bahá Rúḥíyyih Khánum, and recited a few prayers. I had met him in the Holy Land in 1941 for a few minutes, and his radiant countenance is imprinted in my memory.

3. In Winnipeg I was invited to give a talk about the Faith in one of the churches of that city. I accompanied two other Bahá'ís to the church on a Sunday. All those who were present were young, and when the minister guided us to our seats reserved on the first row of benches, the service began. Two American comedians went to the altar and began a comedy show. I asked the minister why such programmes were allowed in the church, and he told me

that it had to be done to attract the young audience, and suggested that I should also include comic stories in my talk to maintain their attention! I told him that in fact my talk was going to be a serious one that day, and he answered that in that case he was not going to be responsible for the consequences.

When it was time for me to speak, I talked for about forty minutes on the history and teachings of the Faith. Everyone listened attentively and at the end of my talk their continuous applause proved their interest. The minister was astonished, and told me that that was the first time the youth had listened so carefully to a serious talk.

4. In the vicinity of Winnipeg there was an Indian reservation and at the time only one Bahá'í family lived there. One day one of the Winnipeg Bahá'ís and I decided to visit this family and together with another Bahá'í began our trip. We drove a few hours, then took a canoe, and then walked for a while before we reached the reservation. A middle-aged man came to greet us and guided us to his cabin. He had a daughter who was ill and in bed on the floor. He asked us to recite the Healing Prayer and immediately opened the windows of his cabin, saying 'Let the words of God travel to other cabins and influence the hearts of the people and add to the number of believers on this reservation.' We were deeply moved, and in utmost supplication recited the Healing Prayer entreating Almighty God for the healing of his daughter.

5. On 30 June 1953, I was taken to visit one of the believers of Hamilton who had been hospitalized in a sanatorium immediately after giving birth to her child. A few Bahá'í books and a collection of prayers were on the table in her room. When I was introduced, she became happy and began to ask a series of questions. First she wanted to know the wisdom of the number ninety-five. I answered that the Master in one of His Tablets had

indicated that the numerical value of the 'Báb' in the Abjad alphabet was five, and this figure, multiplied by the Váḥid, nineteen, would equal ninety-five. Then she asked other questions and I answered them to the best of my ability, while thinking to myself that though ill in bed, with her eight-month-old baby taken from her, she still wished to increase her knowledge of the Writings and penetrate the depth of that Ocean. In my heart, I greatly admired her zeal and devotion. Years later this same believer came to the Holy Land on her pilgrimage and told me that her child was now a handsome young man and a very active and devoted Bahá'í.

The European Intercontinental Teaching Conference

I returned to the United States from Canada, and on 14 July 1953 went to Holland on my way to the third Intercontinental Conference in Stockholm. I had a short visit in that country and, after meeting the friends in a few Bahá'í centres, continued my journey to Sweden and joined my fellow workers there.

The Stockholm Conference, 21–6 July, was held in one of the most prestigious halls of that beautiful city. Almost 400 Bahá'ís from thirty countries, speaking twenty-five languages, attended. The Conference was opened on the morning of 22 July with prayers in several languages. The Hand of the Cause Dr Ugo Giachery, representing the beloved Guardian, read the Guardian's message and talked about the significance of the Ten Year Crusade, calling the believers to arise whole-heartedly. In addition to Dr Giachery, there were present thirteen other Hands of the Cause of God. On the afternoon of the same day, the believers viewed the portrait of the Báb, which was placed on a table covered with a silk cloth with flowers arranged around it. While all the believers stood silently, Dr Giachery unveiled the portrait. He then paid his own respects to the precious gift from the beloved Guardian after which one of the Afnáns recited the Tablet of Aḥmad. Then the believers passed by and in utmost order viewed the portrait. This spiritual march lasted two-and-a-half hours during which time melodious music was played. I recalled the letter that Mírzá Sa'íd K͟hán, the Minister of Foreign Affairs, addressed to the Iranian Ambassador in Istanbul concerning the Bábís, assuring him that, 'Praised be God that by the considerations of His Imperial Majesty the S͟háh, the king of kings, the glorious, the protector of religion – may my spirit be a sacrifice to him – they have been uprooted!' Could he ever imagine that one day, and so soon, the representatives of thirty countries would humbly and reverently pass by the portrait of the Wronged One of the world and the Promised of all nations and bend their heads in their devotion?

In addition to the daytime and evening sessions for the Bahá'ís, a successful and dignified public meeting was held, attended by almost 700 persons.

On the day that contributions were offered to purchase land for future Mas͟hriqu'l-Ad͟hkárs in Stockholm and Frankfurt, the generosity, zeal, and enthusiasm of the believers was truly a scene to see. The believers gave whatever they had, and on the table jewellery including Bahá'í and wedding rings, watches and cameras could be seen. However, my intention is to record my personal memoir, and not an account of these historic events, with their highlights of sixty-three pioneer offers for Europe's share in the World Crusade and the splendid Unity banquet in the beautiful Golden Room of Stockholm's Town Hall. These and the inspiring talks by Hands of the Cause and others are fully reported in *The Bahá'í World* (vol. XII, pp. 167–78). I take the liberty, however, of quoting the summary of my own talk which appeared in this official report:

In beginning his presentation of 'The Dawn-Breakers', Mr 'Alí-Akbar Furútan said that the Guardian had instructed the believers to study the history of the Faith and compare it with the early days of past religions . . . [and] he cited the many examples of absolute obedience in the Bahá'í Faith. One, taken from the record of the last days of the earthly life of the Báb, tells that when the Báb called for a volunteer to take His life (not wishing, as He said, to die by the hand of an unbeliever) a youth sprang to his feet, ready to obey His command and later explained that his obedience was to His Cause, not to His person; to His Word, not to His personality. Mr Furútan closed his remarks by referring to a saying of 'Abdu'l-Bahá: 'A small piece of cotton can prevent the ear from hearing sweet melodies. A very thin veil can cover the eyes and make it impossible for them to see. A very small headache can cause our mind to stop functioning . . . a small drop of mortal poison can kill the person who takes it. The veils of selfishness are like the piece of cotton, the thin veil, the small headache and the drop, but those heroic souls (the Dawn-Breakers) did not let any veils come in between them and their true responsibility.'

Germany, France, Spain, Portugal and Egypt

At the conclusion of the Conference, a cable was received from the beloved Guardian addressed to the Persian Hands of the Cause guiding them to travel through Europe and encourage the friends before attending the final Intercontinental Teaching Conference in India. Therefore, the Hands of the Cause each went to a different country, I first to Germany. There I met the Bahá'ís in important cities such as Hamburg, Frankfurt/Main, Wiesbaden, Ebingen (a goal of their Five Year Plan), Karlsruhe, Freiburg/Br. and Stuttgart, and attended, and very much enjoyed, the Summer School at Esslingen where many of the friends had gathered from different parts of Germany.

In Stuttgart, Frau Annemarie Schweizer, the widow of the late Colonel Friedrich Schweizer, in whose home 'Abdu'l-Bahá stayed while visiting Germany, and who was also privileged to meet the Guardian of the Cause of God in 1934, recounted many of her precious memories of these visits and filled all hearts with joy and enthusiasm.

Also, there is a moving story about Frau Herma Mühlschlegel, the wife of the Hand of the Cause of God, Dr Adelbert Mühlschlegel, which is known in Germany by everyone. It is about a young Persian girl, the daughter of a distinguished pioneer, who was studying in Stuttgart. One day she had an unfortunate accident in which she lost part of her skin. She was taken to the hospital where Dr and Frau Mühlschlegel joined her. When it became apparent that her injury was so critical as to require a skin transplant, Herma Mühlschlegel 'spontaneously offered a portion of her own skin tissue', and for fourteen consecutive days lay next to the young girl, patiently tolerating the excruciating discomfort and pain. This she did to save one member of her human family, and through her sacrifice 'the transplantation succeeded very well'. I visited this Bahá'í student in hospital and heard the story from herself, and when I met Frau Mühlschlegel, I witnessed with my own eyes the extent of her selflessness and devotion and was greatly attracted to the spirit of detachment and sincerity of that true Bahá'í. (See *The Bahá'í World*, vol. XIV, p. 368.)

Years later I again met this same Persian girl, who by then had completed her education and was married, and learned that she had only lost one finger, all else having been successfully treated.

On 23 August I left Germany for France, and visited the Bahá'ís in several cities of that country including Paris, Lyon and Marseilles. Then on 5 September I went on to Spain to meet the friends in Madrid and Barcelona, and continued on to Portugal and the cities of Lisbon and Oporto, where again I was with the believers.

Then via France and Italy I travelled to Egypt. Many meetings were held in Cairo, after which I visited

Alexandria where I met with the Local Spiritual Assembly and the National Youth Committee. Returning to Cairo I consulted the National Spiritual Assembly on the goals of the Ten Year Crusade, and after visiting the devoted and zealous friends of Port Said and Ismailia for a few days, on 5 October I departed for India.

The Asian Intercontinental Conference

The magnificent and glorious fourth Intercontinental Conference in India was held in New Delhi, the capital of that country, 7–15 October, and 325 people were present from twenty-seven countries on the first day. It was 'the first international Bahá'í gathering ever to be held in the East'. By the close of the Conference registration had reached 489 participants from thirty-one countries. The measurable results of this historic occasion were as follows:

1. Seventy-four believers volunteered to pioneer to the goal areas of the Ten Year Crusade, and twenty-five of them left almost immediately. (It was my privilege to speak to these last-mentioned friends, comparing these events to the early days of Christianity, and quoting words of the Master on the spiritual significance of pioneering.)
2. $45,000 was contributed towards the purchase of land for the Mashriqu'l-Adhkárs in New Delhi, Baghdad and Sydney.
3. Almost $10,000 was pledged for the Pioneering Deputization Fund, and two believers promised to bear the expenses of two pioneers for ten years.
4. Contributions were also made for development of the Panchgani Bahá'í School.

These were tangible consequences of the Conference. The intangible and spiritual results cannot be described in terms of numbers or concrete facts, but the messages of the beloved Guardian and the addresses of the speakers generated a spirit of devotion to the goals of the Ten Year Crusade and the onward march of the Faith in the Far East and the islands of the South Pacific. The gathering of those believers, with their different customs, speaking different languages, representing different nations and tribes, yet treating each other more kindly and affectionately than sisters and brothers, was an example of the unity of mankind and an evidence of the unique transforming power of the teachings of Bahá'u'lláh.

My inadequate pen is unable to portray the day that the believers viewed the portrait of the Báb. When the friends of North, Central and South America, Africa, Australia and New Zealand, Europe and eight countries of Asia humbly passed before the portrait, no one could resist the flood of emotions which overcame him. This scene was enough to transport anyone to the realms of the spirit. And at the same time, one praised God that within only a century after the Declaration of the Point of the Bayán, thousands in both the East and the West had been privileged to serve His sacred Threshold, and had taken pride in viewing His blessed portrait.

The Báb in *Dalá'il-i-Sab'ih* (The Seven Proofs) describes the ignorance of those who denied Him, and the heedlessness of those who opposed Him in words such as these:

> . . . Now consider that Presence of God for Whom all have been created. The Mountain of Máh-Kú hath now attained that Presence. Notwithstanding this, all call on His Name, and yet are veiled from Him, and all exert themselves for His sake, yet they are barred from Him . . .

But in that Conference hundreds of the lovers of His Cause solaced their eyes by seeing His radiant Countenance. Verily, praised be our Lord, the Most Exalted, and praised be our Lord, the Glory of Glories.

In addition to the sessions of the Conference, which were

only for Bahá'ís, there were numerous public occasions and contacts for and with non-Bahá'ís. These included:

1. A reception and news conference for over thirty representatives of the local and foreign press in one of the best hotels of New Delhi, the Hotel Imperial.
2. Two magnificent meetings, one held in New Delhi Town Hall, and one where the sessions of the Conference were held, in the grounds of the Constitution Club.
3. A public reception and tea in the garden of the Hotel Imperial attended by about a thousand guests, including a large number of dignitaries of the city, representatives of foreign embassies, high officials of the Indian government, distinguished citizens, and newspaper editors.
4. In addition, delegations representing different Bahá'í communities met on separate occasions with the President, Vice-President and Prime Minister of India, and were warmly greeted. As the Hands of the Cause of God participated, I was also included and witnessed the dignity and glory of the Cause manifested in these meetings, and praised God that the fame of the Cause has spread to that distant land and the Holy Name of Bahá'u'lláh was so befittingly proclaimed.

The climax of the Conference was reached with receipt of a cable from the beloved Guardian announcing the completion of the superstructure of the Shrine of the Báb after years of tremendous labour and devotion on the part of the Bahá'í world community. For us it seemed also to mark the climax of the Holy Year. On 15 October 1953 after nine glorious days, the last session of the Conference was concluded amidst the jubilant feelings of the participants who were inspired by hearing the recorded voices of the Master and Martha Root.

The Hand of the Cause Ugo Giachery, the representative of the Guardian, with Bahá'ís who volunteered for pioneer posts during the European Intercontinental Teaching Conference, Stockholm, July 1953

Bahá'ís attending the Asian Intercontinental Teaching

A public meeting during the Intercontinental Teaching Conference
New Delhi, October 1953

Conference, New Delhi, India, 7–15 October 1953

Some of the Bahá'ís attending the Intercontinental Teaching Conference in New Delhi

Unity Banquet in the Golden Room of Stockholm's Town Hall during the Intercontinental Teaching Conference, Stockholm, July 1953

Fifty-One Days in Australasia

During the last days in New Delhi we received another cable from the beloved Guardian directing the Hands of the Cause of God to travel through different countries after the conclusion of the Conference. I was instructed to go to Australia and New Zealand, and therefore I went to Bombay to prepare for my journey. There I also met with the Bahá'ís, and on 24 October gave a lecture on the proofs of the Revelation of Bahá'u'lláh which was very well received by a large group of Bahá'ís and non-Bahá'ís in one of the assembly halls of that city.

Next day, boarding an English ship, we left Bombay and through the waves of a turbulent Indian Ocean began our crossing to Australia. There were ten of us Bahá'ís on board, eight of whom were Australian. On the second day we gathered to elect three of us to arrange for dawn prayers and teaching activities. Through the efforts of this committee three fireside meetings, one every three days, were held in the social hall of the ship. We had more than fifty seekers on each occasion to whom we distributed Bahá'í pamphlets.

In Colombo, the capital of Ceylon (Sri Lanka), we stopped for a few hours. The passengers disembarked to see the city, while we went to visit the friends in the Ḥaẓíratu'l-Quds. Continuing our journey, we said a prayer as we passed the Cocos Islands for the success of the only pioneer there. Finally, on 5 November 1953 after spending eleven days at sea, we reached Fremantle, a port in Western Australia. (I would also like to mention that when we crossed the Equator, we participated in the traditional ceremonies held on leaving the Northern Hemisphere and entering the Southern.) A few friends had come to greet us, and with them was a reporter from the West Australian newspaper, who asked a few questions about the Faith and published an article on this interview in the next issue of the paper. Later, in nearby Perth, twenty of the friends welcomed us at the Ḥaẓíratu'l-Quds.

The day after our arrival in Australia we travelled to Albany and immensely enjoyed the companionship of devoted and enkindled Bahá'ís of that city. An article had been published beforehand in one of the daily newspapers on the tenets of the Faith and the purpose of our journey to Australia, announcing the date of the public meeting. This meeting was gloriously successful, and the audience was so moved and stirred by the teachings of Bahá'u'lláh that one listener wired a friend of his in Perth recommending him to participate in all the Bahá'í meetings. On 7 November we returned to Perth for another fireside meeting, and two days later left for Adelaide, South Australia, where on the evening of our arrival we conveyed to the friends in a public gathering all the glad-tidings of the Intercontinental Conferences.

Then we began our tour of different localities around Adelaide, meeting the Bahá'ís in places such as Burnside, Lyndoch, Unley, Port Lincoln, Payneham, Cleve, Kapunda and Woodville. Truly the friends in these cities were so attracted to the teachings of the Cause and so imbued with faith and certitude that they forgot their former prejudices, became lovers of mankind and, above all, accepted the station of Muḥammad and understood that the Qur'án is in the same rank as the Bible; in a word, they became a 'new creation'.

In Kapunda we met a German woman who had just become a Bahá'í. Her four-year-old daughter sat with us, crossed her hands, and with her sweet accent recited 'Yá Bahá'u'l-Abhá' three times. The spirituality, devotion, and enkindlement of this mother and daughter moved us so much that tears of joy gathered in our eyes.

On 15 November we left for Melbourne, one of the major cities of Australia, and met with Bahá'ís on the night of our arrival to share with them the news of the Delhi Conference. From there we crossed to Tasmania, an island south of Australia, and arrived in Hobart, its capital city. Two meetings were held here, one for Bahá'ís only and another open to the public, in the Ḥaẓíratu'l-Quds which was located in one of the most beautiful areas of the city. Individual meetings were also arranged with leading Theosophists, in which they expressed their harmony with the teachings of Bahá'u'lláh. We also visited the chairman of the Local Spiritual Assembly who was in hospital, and on the following day were interviewed at two radio stations. Next day we left for Launceston, attending a meeting for Bahá'ís and non-Bahá'ís the same evening in the home of one of the friends. On 20 November we continued our tour to Devonport. There extensive discussions about the Faith were pursued with a number of seekers on the evening of our arrival, including the chairman of the Esperanto Society, a newspaper reporter, and a representative of one of the radio stations. On the following day we met the editor of the local newspaper, had a ten-minute radio interview and then returned to Melbourne.

In Melbourne a large and dignified meeting was held in the home of one of the believers, and the talk on the teachings of Bahá'u'lláh so moved those who were present that one of the seekers gave a lengthy talk praising the tenets and goals of the Bahá'í Faith!

We spent 22 November visiting those believers who, for one reason or another, were not able to attend the meetings, and in the evening celebrated the Nineteen-Day Feast, leaving for Ballarat on the following day. There was only one Bahá'í in this town, a girl of nineteen who had pioneered alone and, because of her friendly personality, had gathered many friends around her. With the efforts of this young girl, a fireside meeting was held in the home of one of the seekers, an article was published in the local newspaper about the Faith, and a ten-minute radio interview on the teachings was given.

While returning to Melbourne we met a non-Bahá'í woman in the train. Her husband was a well-known physician in a major hospital, and she herself was chairman of the Board of Directors of the Society for the Blind. She told me in the course of conversation that she had accompanied her husband to Europe the previous year, but had had an unhappy time away from her own country. I told her that I had been travelling for almost a year in many parts of the world, but had never felt lonely or homesick; she answered sadly that I should not compare myself with her as I was a Bahá'í and had friends regardless of where I went! I said to myself, 'Praise God that an Australian of English origin, in whose empire, as they say, the sun never sets, should envy the happiness of a Persian!' Such is the crown with which Bahá'u'lláh adorned our heads. 'And God aided with His succour whom He would . . . ' (Qur'án III: 2.)

On the morning of 25 November we went to Warrnambool to meet a Bahá'í family who had pioneered there, again returning to Melbourne. As a matter of good fortune, there we met Miss Effie Baker, the believer who on the instructions of the beloved Guardian had travelled throughout Iran to photograph the holy and historical places of the Faith for publication in *The Dawn-Breakers*, the English translation of Nabíl's Narrative. A radio interview which we taped was broadcast that afternoon, bringing happiness to the hearts of the believers. And thus our tour of Australia ended, and we had to bid farewell to all the beloved friends there.

We flew to New Zealand on 27 November in turbulent weather which greatly disturbed the passengers, and after eight hours arrived at Christchurch, South Island. After visiting the friends in that city, we went on to Dunedin and north to Nelson; crossing to North Island we stopped in Wellington, Wanganui, New Plymouth and Auckland, in each place conveying news of the Bahá'í world.

In Dunedin we had an extensive talk on the tenets of the Faith with the editor of one of the major newspapers, who wrote and published a very favourable article. In Wellington two meetings were held in which forty of the city dignitaries were present, and many newspaper articles on the Faith appeared subsequently. In Wanganui we had a radio interview; in New Plymouth a meeting attended by eighteen seekers was arranged, and many interviews were given to newspaper editors which resulted in a number of favourable articles.

We arrived in Auckland on the morning of 3 December, and after meeting with the friends had a radio interview. We then went to Devonport, Birkenhead, and Whangarei where, after seeing the friends, we were interviewed by the reporter of the local newspaper and later talked about the Faith on the radio.

On 5 December a meeting was held for the Bahá'ís in the Auckland Ḥaẓíratu'l-Quds, and in the afternoon we went to Hamilton to attend another large fireside meeting. The following day a magnificent public meeting was held in one of the major halls of the city, many pamphlets being distributed. We returned to Auckland in the afternoon of the same day to bid the friends of New Zealand farewell and our leave-taking in the Ḥaẓíratu'l-Quds was indeed a sorrowful and moving occasion. We flew back to Australia the next day, 7 December 1953.

On the evening of our arrival in the beautiful Ḥaẓíratu'l-Quds of Sydney I was happy to meet again the Hand of the Cause of God Mrs Clara Dunn who had attended the Conference in New Delhi. She and her husband Hyde Dunn had been the first pioneers to Australia, New Zealand and Tasmania, and the beloved Guardian had praised them as true conquerors because they had stayed where they pioneered. (*The Bahá'í World*, vol. XII, p. 862.) A large public meeting was held in the same Centre the next night, which lasted until after midnight. We left Sydney for Brisbane on the 10th and were greeted by reporters and photographers who later published an article about the Faith. The following day we were with the Bahá'ís and seekers, and on 12 December attended the Nineteen-Day Feast, which was followed by yet another fireside. The day after was also devoted to meeting the friends, and a radio interview was taped next day which was later broadcast twice.

On the afternoon of 14 December we left for the industrial town of Ipswich where three hundred workers were present in a meeting; the teachings of Bahá'u'lláh were so appealing to them that their lengthy applause was several times repeated. At the close they took about 150 pamphlets. At 4.00 p.m. of the same day we returned to Brisbane to have a twenty-minute radio interview, and spent the evening at the home of one of the believers enjoying the company of other Bahá'ís. We had another five-minute interview with the National Radio of Australia the following day, and were with other friends in the evening.

Our next stop was Lismore, where we went to the home of the beloved pioneers of that city. Before the meeting which was to be held there that evening, we had a chance to become acquainted with our hosts – a family with three children, two girls and a boy of tender years. The father asked that Persian prayers be read, and I accepted. After the prayer was chanted, I noticed that the younger girl, who was not more than eighteen years old, was crying bitterly. Upon asking why, her mother sadly explained to me that her daughter longed to go pioneering on her own, but that she and her husband did not deem it wise for her to leave at that time. They were themselves pioneers at Lismore, their daughter had not yet reached the legal age of maturity and had not finished her education, but, above all, neither could they afford to support her in her pioneering post nor were they willing to burden the Fund. Her daughter, she continued, did not accept any of these reasons and repeated by day and by night that time was short and she could no longer wait. Her parents asked me to talk to her and try to convince her to postpone her plan. It was truly a difficult situation, but I finally decided to talk to the girl and after the meeting I met her privately. All through my conversation with her, she, with her innocent face and sad eyes, kept insisting on her decision, repeating that there was only a very short time left and she could not wait. She said that the beloved Guardian in his message had charged everyone, young and old, with the responsibility to carry out the goals of the Ten Year Crusade, adding that when Mullá Ḥusayn called on his companions to mount their horses and follow him to the Fort of Ṭabarsí, everyone obeyed. 'What if one of them had not obeyed? How would history have judged him?' she asked.

After this conversation, I advised her parents to leave her to herself and assist her to maintain a tranquil conscience, and then I returned to my hotel. At about 5.00 a.m. someone knocked at my door. It was the girl's father. He apologized for having awakened me, but explained that he had no alternative as his daughter had not stopped crying since we had gone, and they had finally decided to come and see me. I dressed and went to the lobby of the hotel to meet her. Pale in face, she had found a seat in the corner of the lobby and was waiting for me. We had a lengthy conversation, and upon my insistence she finally consented to write to the beloved Guardian and ask his guidance on this matter. She wrote the letter immediately and gave it to me to post.

A few days later, when we attended the Summer School of Australia, I met this same family. I was then intending to post her letter, but she radiantly informed me that her parents had finally given her their consent to pioneer elsewhere, which she did. Later, on my return to Iran when I was reading the incoming mail of the Assembly, I came across news that shook the core of my being. This same young girl had passed away at her pioneering post. It seems that soon after she had arrived there, but not until after she had guided several waiting souls to the Cause, she had fallen ill, and within a few short days her sanctified spirit had winged its flight to the Kingdom of Abhá. Tears flowed down my face. Only then did I realize the wisdom of her insistence that time was short – too short to wait. Previously, I had been unable to understand why an eighteen-year-old girl should be in such haste to pioneer.

To return to my memories of Lismore, we were interviewed by a reporter at his office, when the Faith was discussed in detail. The full content of this interview was given in a comprehensive article published the next day. That same evening there was yet another gathering in which the seekers were much moved by the teachings of the Faith.

On 17 December we returned to Sydney for two public meetings in the Ḥaẓíratu'l-Quds on the 17th and 18th, when large audiences attended. The following day found us in Newcastle with the friends, and in Wagga that evening for a meeting, after which we continued our tour to Wollongong to participate in a public meeting on the evening of 21 December. We returned to Sydney at 6.00 p.m. next day for yet another public meeting in the National Ḥaẓíratu'l-Quds, when I spoke of the Most Great Peace and the events to precede its realization. The evening of 23 December was our last meeting with the friends of Sydney and, after bidding them farewell, we went on to meet the friends in Kalgoorlie.

In summary, from 5 November through 26 December 1953, fifty-one days altogether, we visited forty-two cities and localities where Bahá'ís lived, talked to many seekers, met with many newspaper editors and reporters and had several radio interviews about the Cause of God.

The Yerrinbool Bahá'í Summer School of Australia which I then attended began on 31 December. This institution had been inaugurated eighteen years before, and its several buildings were situated in the midst of a beautiful wooded area. The property was a gift to the Faith from Mr and Mrs Stanley Bolton, outstanding Australian Bahá'ís. After the conclusion of the ten-day session my long journey came to its end, and I returned to Iran via Indonesia, Singapore, India and Pakistan.

Here I should like to quote the letter which I addressed to the National Spiritual Assembly of the Bahá'ís of Australia and New Zealand at the close of this tour:

Very dear friends of Australia and New Zealand:

Alláh'u'Abhá!

Almost two months ago, at the request of the beloved Guardian, I commenced a tour of your beautiful country. During this time I have been able to visit forty-two centres, and I am very happy to say that all are doing their utmost to carry out their spiritual responsibilities, especially in teaching the beloved Cause. There is no doubt that at the present time the Faith is in a stage of rapid progress. In many places I found new believers, and in one community in particular, there were seven enrolments in one week. This shows how the friends have arisen with love and devotion, and have thus drawn to themselves the confirmation, strength and assistance of the Abhá Kingdom.

Dearest friends, we are living in an Age which has been the ardent desire of all the prophets and saints of the past. This Age is the pride of all bygone Ages. This is the Day when the Promised One of all the ages has been made manifest; when the Sun of Truth is shining most resplendently. To express our thanks and gratitude, we must serve so devotedly and enthusiastically that the holy ones of the Kingdom of Abhá will be gladdened by our deeds. At the present time our first consideration must be the fulfilment of the Ten Year Plan. This is a sacred trust of the beloved Master, 'Abdu'l-Bahá. He has set out every detail in His long and numerous tablets, and the beloved Guardian has assigned to each and all of us our share in this Plan. It is a Divine call to *every believer* – young or old – they must ponder on the ways and means by which they can best help in its fulfilment.

In accomplishing this Plan we fulfil the desire of 'Abdu'l-Bahá that the bewildered members of the human family may find shelter under the Divine Tabernacle of love and unity. Now is the time for the sowing of seed; if we are faithful in this, the harvest will be assured.

The Ark of God, though attacked by storms and tempests, is guided by the Master hand, and we who are the dwellers in the Divine Ark know that it is moving steadily and surely, and its safe arrival is assured. Ours is the duty of obeying the Master of the ship, so that the Ark may gain velocity.

Due to the obedience of the friends throughout the world to the call of the Guardian, and the determined efforts they have exerted, the standard of the beloved Faith has now been unfurled in more than 200 countries and territories.

I should like to express my great happiness in witnessing the valiant efforts of the believers in Australia and New Zealand to spread the Divine teachings, and the success of their efforts. Whenever I write to the Holy Land I pass on this good news.

In conclusion, I should like to express my sincere thanks to each and all of you for your kindness and hospitality. The most precious gift that I shall take back to Persia is the recollection of your enthusiasm in the service of our beloved Cause. The friends in Iran will be very happy to hear of your devotion, zeal and service, which I shall personally relate to them – especially to the 30,000 Bahá'ís of Tehran . . .

8

Second Pilgrimage to the Holy Land

Soon after my return to Iran I was again granted the privilege of pilgrimage to Haifa, and in February 1954 travelled to the Holy Land. The period of pilgrimage was by then reduced to nine days.

Generally, the programme for pilgrims from the East was scheduled so that in the mornings the pilgrims visited the Shrine of the Báb, the Archives, and the Monument Gardens; in the afternoons the Bahá'í women went to the House of the Master, while the Bahá'í men remained at the Pilgrim House to meet the Guardian there. The beloved Guardian usually came to the gardens about 4.00 o'clock in the afternoon, and as soon as our eyes caught a glimpse of him coming through the main gate of the garden, we would joyously rush towards him, hearing his compassionate voice advising us: 'Do not tire yourselves. Walk gently.' Then we would follow him into the southern gardens of the Shrine, and as soon as the golden dome could be seen, he would say: 'This edifice is unique. It is not similar to a synagogue, nor to a church or a mosque. It is unique. Unique in the heavens and on the earth.' Then he would walk though the small gate at the end of the diagonal path and towards the cypress trees that mark the place blessed by the footsteps of Bahá'u'lláh. One day he spoke of Bahá'u'lláh's visit to this spot, accompanied by 'Abdu'l-Bahá, and of how the Blessed Beauty had said:* 'Áqá, in future thou must purchase this land, which is very pleasant

* As noted before, the words attributed to the Guardian are as I recalled them later, and are not his exact words.

and has a very good view, and transfer the remains of the Báb from Iran to here.' Therefore, it is not by chance that the Shrine of the Báb is erected on this spot. The Blessed Beauty indicated this location with His blessed finger, and issued His order to transfer the sacred remains of the Báb.

He also told us that the prophecy of Isaiah that the Tabernacle of God will be raised on the Mount of God was an allusion to Bahá'u'lláh's tent which was pitched on Mount Carmel. 'The Bahá'ís should know that the Founder of the Shrine of the Báb is the holy Person of the Blessed Beauty, and the Master was the executor of His Plan.'

After this talk, the Guardian would follow the edge of the garden, walk with the pilgrims for a while, then go down the path on the west side of the Shrine and walk along the terrace to the room of Siyyid Abu'l-Qásim-i-Khurásání, above which was an area prepared to receive the pilgrims. Here he would take his seat and, on his instructions, Dr Luṭfu'lláh Ḥakím would serve tea. Then, as soon as the Shrine of the Báb was illuminated, he would accompany the pilgrims to the Shrines. The Shrines of the Báb and the Master were visited alternately.

The Guardian visited the Shrines in the following manner and, of course, we followed him. Near the entrance door he removed his shoes, entered the holy precincts, knelt and prostrated himself by the Sacred Threshold, and after a while rose to chant the Tablet of Visitation. He then again prostrated himself, arose and, facing the inner Shrine, slowly walked backwards and through the door. Then after another short walk in the gardens, he would go towards the Pilgrim House, and then leave. More or less, we followed this programme every day.

Now I would like to recount a few of my other memories from this second pilgrimage:

1. One day when the beloved Guardian was walking with us in the eastern section of the gardens, and standing in the

The Shrine of the Báb in 1954, after completion of the superstructure the previous October

View in 1953 *from Carmel (now Ben-Gurion) Avenue of the recently completed Shrine of the Báb. The nine terraces below the Shrine are visible above the ornamental gate (centre).*

farthest corner overlooking the city, he talked about the New World Order, stating that the Administrative Order is the nucleus and pattern of the World Order, and the World Order, he said, is the prelude to a Divine Civilization. One of the pilgrims mentioned that the matter was unfamiliar to him, and the beloved Guardian said, 'These principles have been given in detail in my letters. You should study them.'

2. One day after we had visited the Shrine of the Báb, and were walking towards the Pilgrim House, he stopped and faced the pilgrims and said: 'Do you know why I immerse the Shrine of the Báb in light every night? It is to compensate for the dark nights of the prison of Máh-Kú where the blessed Báb was denied even a lantern for nine months.' He then firmly added, 'Who could imagine that His sacred remains would be transferred to the Mountain of God from the edge of the moat of Tabríz? Who could imagine that His Shrine would be erected with such glory and majesty? Such is the power of God. Such is the divine confirmation.'

3. Another day, when the beloved Guardian was standing above the nine terraces, he described the nine other terraces which would be built from the Shrine of the Báb to the top of the mountain, totalling eighteen in all. Each terrace would be named after one of the Letters of the Living, and would be illumined, 'light upon light, light upon light,' he said.

4. One day the beloved Guardian instructed Dr Luṭfu'lláh Ḥakím to show the plan of the buildings that were to be built on the arc. The beloved Guardian had sketched the drawing himself, and had used coloured pencils to distinguish one part from the other. He told us that this sketch was like a sun from which rays radiate. These rays represented the buildings that will be built on the arc facing the resting-places of the Holy Family: the International Archives, the Legislative Centre, the Centre for Interpretation,

and the Centre for Teaching. He only named four institutions at that time.

During the period of our pilgrimage, we, of course, visited all the other holy places, spent two nights in the Mansion of Bahjí, visited the Shrine of Bahá'u'lláh on numerous occasions, visited the Most Great Prison, the House of 'Abbúd, the Mansion of Mazra'ih, the Khán-i-'Avámíd and the Garden of Riḍván, and then returned to Iran.

9

Iran, Turkey and Indonesia: 1954–1957

Upon my arrival in Iran I received a letter from the beloved Guardian directing me to visit Bahá'í centres in that country. In obedience to his instructions I left for Mázindarán on 22 June 1954 and arrived in Bábul the same day. In the evening an illumined gathering was held in the local Ḥaẓíratu'l-Quds, in which the news of the Bahá'í world and the content of the beloved Guardian's words during our last pilgrimage were conveyed to them. We spent the next day visiting the historic places of the Faith, and in the evening participated in another meeting which was attended by the same number of believers, including some from neighbouring villages. Two days later we visited the friends in Ámul, a city famed in Bahá'í history, and returned to Bábul for other gatherings in that city and nearby villages.

In the morning of 2 July we were able to meet the friends of Sárí and its neighbouring villages, staying a second day in Sárí for an evening meeting. On 5 July we had the privilege of visiting Fort Ṭabarsí, seeking assistance in prayer from those sanctified souls who were martyred in the path of God. For two days, 8 and 9 July, meetings were held in the village of Máhfurújak. It is the birthplace of Mullá 'Alí-Ján, who was martyred in Tehran, and whose devoted wife, 'Alavíyyih Khánum, passed away in Máhfurújak. My feeble pen is unable to describe adequately the spirit of devotion, dedication and sacrifice that motivated every believer there.

We then left for Sárí, and for two consecutive nights held evening meetings. We were also able to visit the historical places of that city, before continuing our journey. Soon we received a message that Dr I'timád, chairman of the Local Spiritual Assembly of Sárí, had passed away after a heart attack, and therefore we returned to Sárí immediately for his funeral. A large number of Bahá'ís and non-Bahá'ís, including merchants, physicians and other distinguished individuals, attended this funeral and participated in the ceremony that was held in the Bahá'í cemetery in Máhfurújak. The chanting of the prayers and the speeches of those who spoke of the immortality of the soul and the next worlds of God greatly impressed everyone. Later, many Bahá'ís attended the memorial service held in the house of Dr I'timád.

On 23 July we departed for Sabzivár and had the privilege of visiting the resting-place of the three martyrs of Sháhrúd and other historical places on our way, and arrived in Sabzivár that evening.

Sabzivár, which is designated as Madínatu'l-Khaḍrá (the Verdant City) in the Holy Tablets, was my birthplace and from the beginning of the dawn of the Sun of Reality has been the home of many believers. We spent five days in Sabzivár, visiting the friends on different occasions, and then departed for Níshábúr, the birthplace of the 'Pride of Martyrs' (Badí'), where we arrived that same afternoon.

The Story of Badí'

Níshábúr is not only famous in the long history of Iran and known today for such historic sites as the resting-places of prominent poets of Iran like Shaykh 'Attár and Ḥakím 'Umar-i-Khayyám; it has also a distinguished place in the history of the Faith, and its fame has spread all over the world because of its association with Badí'. So much has been written about him that this humble servant does not consider it necessary to go into great detail in depicting the life of this rare spirit, and only a few lines will be offered the reader.

Badí‘ must have been born about AD 1851 in Ní<u>sh</u>ábúr. This unequalled hero in the arena of sacrifice was not a believer at the time of his meeting with Nabíl-i-A‘ẓam. Although his noble father was one of the survivors of the upheaval at <u>Sh</u>ay<u>kh</u> Ṭabarsí, who was later martyred in Ma<u>sh</u>had in the lifetime of Bahá'u'lláh, Badí‘ became a Bahá'í only after his meeting with Nabíl. However, after declaring his faith, the flames of yearning to attain the presence of Bahá'u'lláh were so enkindled in his heart that he no longer had the patience to remain in his home country, and passionately left Ní<u>sh</u>ábúr for Yazd in the company of <u>Sh</u>ay<u>kh</u> Aḥmad-i-Fáníy-i-Ní<u>sh</u>ábúrí. From there, alone and on foot, he began his journey to Baghdad, and after some time in that city left for Mosul. Later, still on foot, he went on to ‘Akká, met ‘Abdu'l-Bahá in the Mosque of al-Jazzár, and with His guidance twice attained the presence of Bahá'u'lláh. He carried the *Lawḥ-i-Sulṭán* (Tablet of the King) to Náṣiri'd-Dín <u>Sh</u>áh, and was subsequently martyred in July 1869.

In *Bihjatu'ṣ-Ṣudúr* there is an account of the life of Badí‘, related by Ḥájí <u>Sh</u>áh-Muḥammad-i-Amín, the gist of which is briefly as follows. Áqá Buzurg, who was later known as Badí‘, attained the presence of Bahá'u'lláh and then went to Haifa. The Ancient Beauty had given Jináb-i-Amín a small box, which was one-and-a-half *<u>Sh</u>ibr* (*<u>Sh</u>ibr* is the space between the tip of the thumb and that of the little finger) in length, a little less than a *<u>Sh</u>ibr* in width, and one-quarter of a *<u>Sh</u>ibr* deep, to give to Badí‘ in Haifa together with a few lira as provision for his journey. Jináb-i-Amín did not know what the box contained. He met Badí‘ in Haifa and gave him the glad-tidings that he had a trust for him and a bounty had been bestowed upon him. They went outside the town where Jináb-i-Amín delivered the box. Badí‘ held it with his two hands, kissed it, prostrated himself, took the box and a sealed envelope from Jináb-i-

Amín, and walked twenty or thirty steps away from him. He then sat facing the Prison where Bahá'u'lláh was incarcerated and opened the envelope. As soon as he read the Tablet it contained, his face became illumined with joy and he prostrated himself again. Jináb-i-Amín asked Badí' whether he could also read the Tablet, but Badí' replied that there was no time. Jináb-i-Amín sensed that there was something that had to remain a secret, and suggested that they both go into Haifa so that he could give him a sum of money. Badí' refused and said he would not go to the town, but Jináb-i-Amín could go and bring it. When Jináb-i-Amín returned, Badí' was gone, and his search proved to be of no avail. He wrote to Beirut to give the sum of money to Badí' when he reached there, but they also did not see him. Jináb-i-Amín relates that 'We never heard from him again until we received the news of his martyrdom in Tehran and learned that the box contained the Tablet of the King, and the envelope a Tablet to the messenger himself, giving him the glad-tidings of the eventual martyrdom of that essence of constancy and steadfastness'. He also recounts that Jináb-i-Ḥájí 'Alí accompanied Badí' from Trebizond to Tabríz, and witnessed that he was very cheerful, smiling and patient. He knew only that this young man had attained the presence of the Blessed Beauty and was on his way to his home in Khurásán. Jináb-i-Ḥájí also said that he observed Badí' on several occasions; he would walk about one hundred steps, stop, go aside, face the Prison City, prostrate himself and say, 'O God! Do not retrieve by Thy justice what Thou hast bestowed by Thy mercy, and grant Thou me strength to protect it.'

The Journey Continues

After two bountiful days in Níshábúr visiting the friends of the Merciful Lord, we left for Mashhad the next morning, arrived there about noon, and spent all the afternoon and evening hours with individual Bahá'ís. The next night a meeting was held in the home of one of the believers. We talked about the goals of the Ten Year Crusade, the Intercontinental Teaching Conferences, and the enthusiastic response of the Bahá'ís of the world to these goals. This news enlightened the friends and brought much joy to their hearts. There was a similar meeting a day later, followed by a special gathering for the youth. We then attended a fireside meeting arranged for seekers of the truth.

The following two days were also spent in Mashhad, and we had the bounty of being with the junior youth and Bahá'í children and were immersed in an ocean of joy and happiness. On the third day we left for Bushrúyih. Our arrival coincided with the time when the persecution of the friends had intensified, and a few Bahá'ís had had to leave town. We reached the vicinity of the city about midnight. It was very hot, and the city was completely silent. We walked for a while until we reached an alley that led to a covered corridor. A lantern was giving a weak light and we went towards it. Two Bahá'ís were expecting us and took us to a house. In the courtyard the believers had gathered, and as soon as they saw us, like unto people who mourned the loss of their beloved ones, they began to weep with such a weeping that we began to cry too. Then whatever could be done to calm their hearts was done, and the news of the Bahá'í world and the victories of the followers of the Lord of the World in five continents were conveyed to them. Afterwards a few of the believers gave accounts of the persecutions inflicted upon the friends of that town, immersing us all in an ocean of sorrow. This gathering continued until dawn, and after it was adjourned we were taken to the home of one of the believers to rest for a while.

A week later we continued our tour, visiting the friends in several places. In the afternoon of 22 August, we travelled on donkeys to two remote villages, and passing through the mountains and valleys reached the first village and were housed in the home of one of the Bahá'ís. A pleasant day was spent visiting the friends and mentioning the Name of God, and then we continued on to the neighbouring village. On the first evening we attended the meeting of the Local Spiritual Assembly, and then a meeting of all the believers. Similar gatherings were held the next two nights, and on the morning of the fourth day we mounted our donkeys again to go to the village of 'Alí-Ábád. On our way, we were most warmly received in several of the gardens and farms of the believers.

Our guide was one of the steadfast friends, and while we were passing through that beautiful valley with its sweetly sounding river and mountain ranges on both sides, he in his soft local accent asked me many profound questions on the seven stages of the Cause named by the beloved Guardian, which I had discussed in a meeting. His questions were so precise and to the point that I was greatly astonished, and inwardly praised God for the miracles that His Cause has performed, exalting His lowly servants like ourselves to such an eternal glory. 'Knowledge is a light which God sheddeth into the heart of whomsoever He willeth.' (An Islamic tradition cited in the *Kitáb-i-Íqán*, p. 184.)

In the afternoon of the same day we arrived in 'Alí-Ábád, took our car which we had left there and drove to Mashhad, which we reached on 27 August. Here we spent our time attending many meetings and firesides, youth and Bahá'í teachers' gatherings and the Summer School, and on 8 October sadly bade the friends farewell and continued our journey to Níshábúr. After three more days and another three in Sabzivár, where our nights and days were spent in gatherings with the friends which greatly benefited us, we left for Tehran, the 'Mother of the World'. Our journey through these cities, towns and villages of Iran lasted almost four months, and was thus happily and safely concluded.

A Mission in Nayríz

A few days after my arrival in Tehran an instruction was received from the beloved Guardian dispatching me immediately to Nayríz, and directing me to exert my utmost efforts to encourage and reassure the steadfast friends of that city who for years have been the target of severe persecution. I left Tehran, therefore, on the morning of 30 October 1954 and arrived in Iṣfahán that afternoon. A meeting was held in the local Ḥaẓíratu'l-Quds, after which I continued my trip next morning to Ábádih to participate in a meeting with the Bahá'ís. Next morning I left for Shíráz.

As the only road to Nayríz, which was unpaved, was closed due to severe rainfall, I was compelled to remain in Shíráz for many days. During this time a great number of occasions were arranged in which I was able to meet adult Bahá'ís, youth and children in both the Ḥaẓíratu'l-Quds and the homes of the friends, as well as in fireside meetings. These continued until the rain stopped and the road to Nayríz was opened, when in the company of a few friends we continued our journey to Nayríz and finally arrived in that city so renowned in Bahá'í history.

We spent twenty-five days in Nayríz. All the hours of our days and nights were spent in meeting the friends. Many classes were arranged, several discussion groups formed, many meetings were held for the Bahá'ís, and in the meantime we tried to visit the historical places of the city. Since it was no longer wise to remain in Nayríz, we sorrowfully bade the friends farewell and left for Tehran, stopping again on the way in Shíráz, Ábádih, and Iṣfahán to remind these communities of their responsibilities towards fulfilling their share of the goals of the Ten Year Crusade.

Dr Luṭfu'lláh Ḥakím, who was then the Persian secretary of the International Bahá'í Council, on the instruction of the beloved Guardian responded to my report of the Nayríz visit as follows: '. . . He [the beloved Guardian] said: "I will pray for the Bahá'ís of Nayríz. Now it is necessary for Mr Furútan to remain in Tehran . . ."'

Persecutions of 1955

In the month of Ramaḍán 1955, a certain Shaykh Muḥammad Taqí, known as Falsafí, suddenly began to make slanderous remarks in one of the mosques of Tehran about the Bahá'ís and their beliefs, and as these speeches were repeated every day, the whole country became threateningly agitated. The friends in all parts of the country were also very troubled, and the National Spiritual Assembly, therefore, began its continuous effort to petition to government authorities to clarify the stand of the Bahá'ís on different issues. This situation continued for a while until the National Convention was held during the Riḍván Festival. The delegates came from every corner of the country to discharge their duties, but on the twelfth day of Riḍván, during the last session of the Convention, orders were received from the military command to suspend the meeting and close the Ḥaẓíratu'l-Quds. The delegates left to gather later in the home of one of the believers. There they concluded their consultation, and after the chanting of many prayers returned to their homes.

On 7 May 1955 the Ḥaẓíratu'l-Quds in Tehran was closed, and subsequently a flood of unwholesome news was received from different Bahá'í centres. The National Spiritual Assembly continued unwaveringly to petition the government authorities, but to no avail. In the month of August 1955, the dome of the National Ḥaẓíratu'l-Quds was demolished, with the participation of army officers watched by a crowd of curious people, and all the other Ḥaẓíratu'l-Quds throughout the country were seized from the Bahá'ís. The Army occupied the National Office and moved their headquarters to it. After these events, the severity of persecutions declined, the month of Muḥarram passed with no major incidents, and gradually all Ḥaẓíratu'l-Quds were returned to the Bahá'ís. The tragic deaths of seven martyrs of Hurmuzak occurred in this same sorrowful year.

Glimpses of Turkey

In May 1956 the beloved Guardian instructed me to travel to Turkey. This journey lasted several months, during which many cities such as Istanbul, Ankara, Izmir, Adana, Gaziantep, Adrianople and Konya were visited. In each of these cities I met the friends, and many deepening classes for the youth were arranged. As I am familiar with the Turkish language, teaching in these classes was relatively easy.

One of my privileges during this trip was to visit a number of the places associated with the history of the Faith in that country, especially the House of Bahá'u'lláh in Adrianople. I also saw the fantastic palaces of the rulers of the Ottoman Empire, including the Palace of Dolmabaçhe on the Bosporus in Istanbul. I had seen many beautiful and magnificent buildings, but the grandeur and elegance of this palace, which was built by Western architects in 1853, was truly dazzling.

The director of the Palace, as I was his guest on the recommendation of some of the Bahá'ís, kindly showed me its various rooms and halls. When we entered the Coronation Hall, he jokingly asked whether I wished to sit on the throne of Sultan 'Abdu'l-'Azíz. 'I am a Bahá'í,' I replied, and explained that Bahá'u'lláh had called it the 'throne of tyranny', adding that Sultan 'Abdu'l-'Azíz was the tyrant king who had banished Bahá'u'lláh, His family and His followers first from Baghdad to Constantinople, next to Adrianople, and then to 'Akká, treating them with utmost tyranny and oppression. As one of the followers of Bahá'u'lláh I could not degrade myself by ascending that throne. The director, who was a knowledgeable man and learned in history, agreed with me and added that some of the sultans of the Ottoman Empire, and particularly 'Abdu'l-'Azíz and 'Abdu'l-Ḥamíd, were tyrannical, bloodthirsty, corrupt and cruel, and had finally been duly punished and wiped from the face of the earth. I praised God at that time for having witnessed the fulfilment of the prophecy of the *Kitáb-i-Aqdas* with my own eyes, and for having heard the condemnation of the actions of the Ottoman Sultans by their own fellow countryman.

It was to 'Abdu'l-'Azíz that Bahá'u'lláh had addressed, while in Adrianople, words of supreme counsel for those who rule over men, counsel which the Sultan wholly ignored. (See *The Proclamation of Bahá'u'lláh*, pp. 47–54.) In little more than fifty years the Sultanate had disappeared; the following is a brief summary of its downfall.

Sultan 'Abdu'l-'Azíz ascended the throne of the Ottoman Empire in 1861, and was deposed and assassinated in 1876. After a three-month reign by Murád V, Sultan 'Abdu'l-Ḥamíd II succeeded; he was hated by his people and deposed in 1909, dying in 1918 in utmost misery, lonely and isolated. He was followed as Sultan by Muḥammad V and nine years later Muḥammad VI came to the throne. The latter, in 1922, fled Turkey upon the abolition of the Sultanate on 1 November by the National Assembly in Ankara, his nephew 'Abdu'l-Majíd, the son of Sultan 'Abdu'l-'Azíz, being kept only as Caliph, or spiritual head of Islam. But on 3 March 1924 the Caliphate was also abolished and Turkey's last sultan was forced to leave his country. Meanwhile, on 29 October 1923 the Republic of Turkey had been proclaimed and the next day Mustafa Kamal Pasha was elected its first President, Ankara becoming its capital. Thus, with one stroke in March 1924, the hereditary rule of the descendants of 'U<u>th</u>mán was abolished, as was the Caliphate itself, and in the next five years the complete secularization of the state was accomplished. In the words of the beloved Guardian, the 'disappearance of the caliph, the spiritual head of above two hundred million Muḥammadans, brought in its wake . . . the annulment of the shari'ah canonical Law, the disendowment of sunní institutions, the promulgation of a civil Code, the suppression of religious orders . . .' The Caliphate had, in his words, 'vanished at a stroke . . .' (See *The Promised Day Is Come*, pp. 95–9.) And thus, for the first time in the history of Turkey, State and religion were separated.

The First Convention of South-East Asia

In October 1953 the Guardian had given to the National Spiritual Assembly of India, Pakistan and Burma the responsibility of establishing the first Regional Spiritual Assembly of South-East Asia, one of sixteen new National and Regional Assemblies to be formed in 1956 and 1957. He had bestowed on me the bounty of representing him in Jakarta at the first Convention, which opened on 30 April 1957. It was my last international journey under the direction of the beloved of all hearts.

Leaving Tehran I passed through Karachi where I met the believers for a few days. In Jakarta I found Bahá'ís from all parts of Asia. Dr Raḥmatu'lláh Muhájir, Knight of Bahá'u'lláh for the Mentawei Islands of Indonesia, participated in the Convention and was accompanied by sixteen others, including the first believer of Mentawei.

The Convention was beautiful both in spirit and organization, and received a Six Year Plan for South-East Asia with enthusiasm. One of the first actions of the newly-formed Regional Assembly was to formulate detailed plans for attainment of the goals in each territory within its jurisdiction. In his message to the Convention the Guardian had described the potentialities of South-East Asia in these words:

By virtue of its vastness, its heterogeneous character, its geographical position, bridging the gulf separating the Bahá'í communities now firmly established in both the northern and southern regions of the Pacific Ocean, the spiritual receptivity of many of its inhabitants, and the role which they are destined to play in the future shaping of the affairs of mankind, this vast area . . . is bound . . . to exercise a far-reaching influence on the future destinies of the World Bahá'í Community . . . (*The Bahá'í World*, vol. XIII, p. 302.)

Within the next two years in Indonesia, which until 1950 had lacked even one Bahá'í, mass teaching began with the trebling of the number of Bahá'ís and the increase of localities with believers to 150. This process was particularly startling in Mentawei, but Vietnam, the Philippines, Sarawak and Brunei grew rapidly in the next five years. Here is a summation of the impressive developments following so soon after the establishment of this first Regional Spiritual Assembly of South-East Asia:

Although the rise of the Faith in the Pacific was everywhere glorious, South-East Asia outran its sister communities, brought untold joy to the Guardian's heart, and in the closing months of the Crusade rivalled Central and East Africa and India. (ibid. pp. 303–4.)

I returned to Tehran via Pakistan and Afghanistan, where I spent a few hours in the airport at Herat.

10

The Passing of the Guardian

The receipt of two messages from the beloved Guardian dated 4 June and October 1957 – in which, in the first, the necessity was emphasized of mutual collaboration between the Hands of the Cause and the National Spiritual Assemblies for the purpose of safeguarding and stimulating the Bahá'í world community and the people of Bahá in the years to come, and, in the second, the glad-tidings of the appointment of eight other dedicated believers to the rank of Hands of the Cause of God was announced, the Hands being instructed to appoint an additional Auxiliary Board charged with the specific duty of 'watching over the security' of the Faith – brought endless happiness and joy to the friends but also greatly vexed their hearts. For, from these instructions, the signs of the separation of the beloved Guardian, the Sign of God, from his devoted followers were visible. But no one could believe that after only a short period of time the sun of beauty of that kind and compassionate Guardian would set, and tears of grief and sorrow would flow from the eyes of those who, life in hand, had dedicated themselves to the Cause he so cherished.

On the morning of 5 November 1957 I received a cable that violently shook the core of my being and benumbed me. In that cable, Amatu'l-Bahá Rúḥíyyih Khánum announced to the Bahá'í world the news of the passing of the beloved Guardian.

Madly I rushed to the home of Miss Adelaide Sharp and gave her the cable. When she had read it, she sat in a corner dumbfounded. After a few minutes, we consulted on the ways by which we should inform the members of the National Spiritual Assembly and the Local Spiritual Assembly of Tehran, and finally decided to call a meeting at 4.00 p.m. of the same day, and cautiously convey to them the news of this greatest calamity. At the appointed time eighteen members were present in the humble dwelling of Miss Sharp. When the news was communicated to them, at first they did not believe it, and then when they were convinced, they were overtaken by such anguish and grief as words are inadequate to describe. It would suffice for readers to turn to their own inner feelings to imagine the distress of the souls of those who were present at that meeting.

The next morning we received another cable from Amatu'l-Bahá inviting the members of the assemblies, and those believers who were able, to attend the funeral of the beloved Guardian. After much consultation in the National Spiritual Assembly, it was decided that I should stay in Tehran to attend the memorial services in that city. Several of these were held in Tehran and its suburbs, each attended by a great number of believers. I needed to be consoled myself, but did my best to talk to the believers, striving to assuage their grief-stricken hearts. The following paragraphs are the essence of my talks in these memorial services.

Beloved friends, from the Declaration of the Most Exalted Countenance (the Báb) until the present time, one hundred and thirteen years have passed. During this period, many momentous events and several tragic crises have taken place that have subjected the followers of the Lord of the World to either exultation or grief. However, by the testimony of friends and foes alike, not one of the afflictions has had the power to prevent the people of Bahá from carrying out the wishes of their Beloved, nor has it been able to undermine the progress of the Cause of God.

After the martyrdom of the Báb, the Sun of the Beauty of Bahá rose from the horizon of the dungeon of Tehran, and after His Declaration in the Garden of Riḍván, notwithstanding His exiles from place to place, and a myriad of afflictions that were imposed upon Him for the period of thirty-nine years, He guided this wronged community in such wise, and exalted the Cause of God to such glory and majesty, that everyone was awestruck, and the enemies and adversaries of the Cause once again lost hope. Two powerful governments of that day, namely, the oppressive and tyrannical Government of Iran, and the proud Sultan of the Ottoman Empire, found themselves defeated when confronting the glory of the Cause.

After the ascension of the Ancient Beauty, as soon as a glimmer of hope to disperse the friends of God was again enkindled in the hearts of the vindictive enemies, the Centre of His Covenant, 'Abdu'l-Bahá, took the helm of the Ship of God in His able hands and guided it to the shore of victory and triumph. He raised the fame of the Cause of God in the West, and did not grant an opportunity to the adversaries of the Faith to rejoice in the realization of their machinations.

After the ascension of the Master to the Most Exalted Kingdom, the Guardian of the Cause of God, the able and mighty lord of the people of Bahá, in the course of thirty-six years of his ministry, propagated the Faith of Bahá'u'lláh in both the West and the East to such an extent that the eyes of those who comprehend were dazzled.

The past is the mirror of the future. We trust, with no hesitation or doubt, that the ascension of the beloved Guardian to the Kingdom of Abhá is in conformity with the wisdom of God, and in itself will move the believers to rush to the arena of service, pioneering, and sacrifice to promote the Cause of God.

11

Chief Stewards: 1957–1963

Soon after the passing of the beloved Guardian, Amatu'l-Bahá Rúḥíyyih Khánum invited all the Hands of the Cause of God to the Holy Land to attend the first Conclave of the Hands and consult on the future of the blessed Cause. Therefore, I too went to that sacred land, and on 17 November joined my colleagues in Haifa.

Twenty-six of the twenty-seven Hands of the Cause were present, and only Mrs True, due to her advanced age, was absent. On 18 November the Hands gathered together in the Mansion of Bahjí for a memorial meeting when many prayers were said in remembrance of the beloved Guardian, after which all the Hands entered the Shrine of Bahá'u'lláh, each one prostrating himself at His Threshold 'in utter humility', supplicating for the protection of the Cause and the unity of the Bahá'í community.

Later, when we had returned to the Mansion for our consultation, I read again to myself for the tenth time the June and October 1957 messages of the beloved Guardian and especially meditated upon these words:

The security of our precious Faith, the preservation of the spiritual health of the Bahá'í communities, the vitality of the faith of its individual members, . . . the fulfilment of its ultimate destiny, all are directly dependent upon the befitting discharge of the weighty responsibilities now resting upon the members of these two institutions [the Hands and National Assemblies] . . . (4 June.)

This latest addition [the 'designation of yet another contingent of the Hands'] to the band of the high-ranking officers of a fast evolving World Administrative Order . . . calls for, in view of the recent assumption by them of their sacred responsibility as protectors of the Faith, the appointment by these same Hands, in each continent separately, of an additional Auxiliary Board, equal in membership to the existing one, and charged with the specific duty of watching over the security of the Faith . . . (October.)

My heart was assured, my mind enlightened, and my soul consoled, and I knew then that the Cause of God would always be protected.

On 25 November the 'Proclamation by the Hands of the Cause to the Bahá'ís of East and West' was sent out. (See *The Bahá'í World*, vol. XIII, pp. 341–5.) Among other momentous paragraphs, it announced that a body of nine Hands would serve at the Bahá'í World Centre to protect the Faith from any attack reported by other Hands or by National or Regional Assemblies, 'correspond with National Assemblies on matters connected with the prosecution of the objectives of the Ten Year Plan' and assist National Assemblies 'on matters involving administrative questions' by citing passages from the Bahá'í sacred literature. As a separate action that day, the Hands of the Cause named the members of this body of nine, and I was among those chosen to serve in Haifa. And so my wife came from Tehran and we settled in Haifa at the World Centre of the Faith.

Later, when in 1958 the Hands of the Cause arrived at their decision to elect the Universal House of Justice in 1963, a surge of joy overtook the hearts and souls of everyone, and all our thoughts were then focused on the winning of the goals of the Ten Year Crusade, the last of the beloved Guardian's wishes. Prayers and supplication at the Holy Shrines were the spiritual food of the Hands of the Cause of God at that time.

The opposition of a small group to the Will and Testament of 'Abdu'l-Bahá disturbed the friends for a while, but these opposing voices gradually became silent, their machinations were completely forgotten, and the meaning of this blessed verse of the Qur'án became evident: '. . . an evil tree pulled up from the earth's surface; it has no stability.' (Mauláná Muḥammad 'Alí translation, XIV: 26.)

During the incumbency of the Hands, the beloved friends and the National Assemblies, praised be God, exerted their utmost efforts to achieve the goals of the Ten Year Crusade, and news of fresh victories was constantly received in the Holy Land and consoled the grief-stricken hearts of those who were residing there.

For a summary of the responsibilities of the Hands of the Cause of God as Chief Stewards and Custodians of the Bahá'í Faith, during these anxious yet triumphant years between the passing of the Guardian and the election of the Universal House of Justice, I can do no better than quote two paragraphs from a survey published in *The Bahá'í World* (vol. XIV, p. 467):

> For nearly five-and-a-half years following the tragic loss of the beloved Guardian, the Hands of the Cause of God, acting in their assigned role as Custodians of the Bahá'í Faith, had effectively managed the affairs of the Cause, bringing into being in 1961 the first elected International Bahá'í Council, guiding the Bahá'ís of the world toward the achievement of a triumphant conclusion of the Guardian's Ten Year Crusade, calling for the election of the first Universal House of Justice, and providing for the celebration of the Most Great Jubilee in London at Riḍván, 1963.
>
> Their sterling efforts during that awesome and critical period in the history of the Faith moved the Universal House of Justice to pay special tribute to the Hands of the Cause in its first message, on the occasion of the World Congress. With the election of the Universal House of Justice they could lay down the heavy administrative burdens which had been thrust upon them in November, 1957, and concentrate their energies on their specialized duties of protection and propagation.

Travels from the World Centre, 1959–1962

After the close of the Conclave of the Hands of the Cause at Bahjí, October–November 1959, I departed for Turkey where I spent six months, through April 1960, travelling to the cities where Bahá'ís lived. During the next few years I was privileged to return to Turkey several times as will be noted in later pages.

The following November I participated, with six fellow Hands, in the joyful and impressive ceremony of laying the foundation stone of the Mother Temple of Europe, on a hilltop in Langenhain outside Frankfurt-am-Main. Nearly one thousand Bahá'ís were present as the Hand of the Cause Amelia Collins read the message from the Hands in the Holy Land and placed in the foundation the precious dust from the Shrine of Bahá'u'lláh. We also attended and addressed a large conference of European Bahá'ís in Frankfurt. In December I visited the newly-formed Bahá'í group in Padova, Italy.

One aspect of the plan of action formulated by the Hands at the 1959 Conclave, to assure the election of the Universal House of Justice in 1963, was their 'call for the election in Riḍván, 1961, of the twenty-one National Spiritual Assemblies of Latin America . . . ' My share, as representative of the World Centre, was to attend the first Conventions of Brazil and Uruguay in Rio de Janeiro and Montevideo, present the message of the Hands of the Cause of God, and witness the formation of their National Spiritual Assemblies. My contributions to the Convention sessions included statements on Bahá'í administration, individual and social aspects of Bahá'í life, teaching and pioneering, child education and the spiritual development of Latin America. The Convention in Brazil was blessed by the presence of Leonora Holsapple Armstrong who, inspired by the Master's Tablets of the Divine Plan, had pioneered to that country in 1921. There were, in addition to the sessions, a number of meetings of Bahá'ís and non-Bahá'ís, to whom I spoke about the fulfilment of the prophecies of the Holy Books, the coming of the Promised One of all religions and nations, and the new teachings of God for this age. I also stopped in Argentina to see the friends of Buenos Aires, and visited the illumined resting-place of Mrs May Maxwell.

On my way to these historic Conventions I had stopped in Britain, where from 5 to 17 April I visited the friends in Wales, the Midlands and the South of England. There was also a meeting in London with Iranian believers from all over the country. Before leaving the United Kingdom it was my privilege to consult with the National Spiritual Assembly as well.

In Cardiff, the capital city of Wales and its 'pivotal centre' as the beloved Guardian called it, I was the guest of a Bahá'í family, a couple with two children, a son of nine and a daughter of eleven years old. We gathered one evening to plan my departure the next morning. I had to be at the train station by 4.00 a.m., and the weather was very cold with heavy snow on the ground. The children insisted on accompanying us, but their parents advised them against this as it was too cold and too early to rise at that time of the morning, and they had to be on time for school.

When I left my room in the morning, however, I saw those two children dressed and ready to go with us. Eventually their parents consented that they come. A few other believers, including Charles Dunning, a radiant older believer who was the Knight of Bahá'u'lláh for the Orkney Islands, had also come to the station to bid me farewell. My intention in recounting this story is to show how the Cause of God has transformed the practical people of the West, adults and children alike, who demonstrated such kindness and consideration to an Easterner whom they had never seen before.

The Hand of the Cause Amelia Collins, representing the Bahá'í World Centre, addressing the Hands of the Cause and believers on the occasion of laying the foundation stone of the Mother-Temple of Europe, Langenhain, near Frankfurt/Main, Germany, 20 November 1960

The first National Spiritual Assembly of the Bahá'ís of Brazil Riḍván 1961

The first National Spiritual Assembly of the Bahá'ís of Uruguay, Riḍván 196

During my return to Haifa I also had the bounty of visiting Cyprus and meeting the beloved Persian pioneers, the Turkish and a few of the Cypriot believers in several gatherings. Their spirit was a miracle of Bahá'u'lláh, for they were as close to each other as members of one family, without a trace of the national prejudices so evident in their fellow countrymen.

The annual Conclave of the Hands, gathered at the Mansion of Bahjí in the autumn of 1961, issued a momentous message on 5 November to the Bahá'ís of East and West announcing that a Convention would be held in the Holy Land for the election of the Universal House of Justice in the first three days of Riḍván 1963. Moreover, due to conditions affecting the Cause in the Middle East, the World Congress would be held in London during the last five days of this Riḍván period. 'It must be a consolation to every believer who plans to be present on this unique occasion', the Hands stated, 'to know that he will be able to visit the grave of Shoghi Effendi and offer his prayers there as the last, majestic, glorious, globe-conquering Plan of his Guardian draws to a close.'

Yet another decision reported in this message was that 'all the Hands, including those resident in the Holy Land, will devote as much of their time as possible to accelerating the process of mass conversion on the one hand, and on the other, in fulfilment of the Guardian's instructions, to meeting frequently with various National Assemblies in order to deliberate with them on ways and means of winning the goals of the Crusade.' Although, as a Hand resident in Haifa I took part in guiding and speaking with pilgrims, who in this year for the first time had the bounty of visiting the beautiful new International Archives, I also assisted in Europe soon after the close of the Conclave. From the end of December into the first week of January 1962, I attended the Austrian Winter School in Matzleinsdorf on the Danube River near Melk. Lively consultation with the fifty believers and six inquirers developed as we discussed a wide variety of topics important to the progress of the Cause. I also much enjoyed meeting the Bahá'í youth in Florence.

12

My First Journeys under the Auspices of the Universal House of Justice

Riḍván of 1963 finally arrived, and the members of the National Spiritual Assemblies from all over the world gathered in Haifa to elect the first Universal House of Justice, the supreme legislative body ordained by Bahá'u'lláh in His Most Holy Book.

The election was held on the morning of 21 April in the House of the Master. After the Convention had been opened with the recitation of prayers in different languages, Amatu'l-Bahá Rúḥíyyih Khánum spoke of the significance of that historic day and explained the method of the election. Then the delegates comprising members of fifty-one National and Regional Spiritual Assemblies who had been able to come to Haifa, numbering 288 believers (ballots had also been received from absent delegates, including those from the five Assemblies unable to be represented in person), proceeded to cast their ballots with that dignity and composure which always characterizes the Bahá'í communities, and is a sign of the World Order of Bahá'u'lláh.

Other sessions of the Convention were held in Beit Harofe, one of the halls in Haifa on Mount Carmel which is situated only a few hundred metres from the arc designed and inaugurated by the Guardian for the World Administrative Centre. When the names of the members of the first Universal House of Justice were announced and they came to the stage, visibly stunned by the news, the joy of the participants in that glorious gathering reached its peak. A few days later in London, the Hand of the Cause Paul E. Haney reported on the election to the participants at the World Congress, saying, 'we were privileged to witness one of the great events of history taking place before our eyes . . . When the balloting was completed, every one felt that Bahá'u'lláh had indeed been present in that gathering and that a unique and wonderful pattern had been established for the world to marvel at and, in the fullness of time, to follow.' (*The Bahá'í World*, vol. XIV, pp. 427–9.)

The account of the Bahá'í World Congress – 'that Most Great, that Wondrous Jubilee' (Shoghi Effendi, 23 November 1951) – held in the Royal Albert Hall in London, which was attended by twelve Hands of the Cause of God, the nine members of the first Universal House of Justice, and more than 6,000 believers, is published in detail in several Bahá'í publications, and it is a certainty that my dear readers have reviewed these articles. A comprehensive report with photographs is given in *The Bahá'í World* (vol. XIV, pp. 57–79). Briefly, this grand and glorious Congress lasted five days from 28 April to 2 May, and with its all-embracing programme was managed in an amazingly organized fashion. Hands of the Cause of God, members of the Universal House of Justice, and a few of the scholars and speakers of the Faith were included in its programme, and a public meeting was also arranged to delineate in full the principles of the Faith for seekers. The presentation of the members of the Universal House of Justice on the afternoon of the second day thrilled the hearts of all present, and the reading of its first message to the Bahá'í world with its tribute to the Hands of the Cause of God who had 'kept the ship on its course and brought it safe to port' was a source of happiness to the Chief Stewards after the anxious years from 1957. There was also an interview arranged in London with national television, in which the teachings of Bahá'u'lláh were discussed. Of course, the participation of

The Hands of the Cause of God on the steps of the House of 'Abdu'l-Bahá, just before the first election of the Universal House of Justice, Riḍván 1963

The Bahá'í World Congress held in the Royal Albert Hall, London, 28 April–2 May 1963

hundreds of believers from different nationalities and races all wearing Congress badges, in itself, was an indirect testimony to the universality of the Faith.

In early 1965 I made my first journey under the auspices of the Universal House of Justice. Initially in Turkey and particularly in Iskenderun, and later in Iran, many Bahá'ís were visited and encouraged to prosecute the objectives of the first Nine Year Plan (1964–1973) of that Supreme Body. This journey lasted a few months and, praised be God, with His assistance and confirmation proved to be very fruitful.

In 1967 I went to India, travelled to important centres of that vast sub-continent, and had the bounty of visiting many of the devoted friends of that land. In addition to the numerous meetings, I visited the Vice-President of India and the Minister of Education, was interviewed by several newspaper reporters, and attended many fireside gatherings. In all of these the exalted principles and the spiritual and social teachings of the Faith were discussed.

In Gwalior, a city of half a million people in north central India in the province of Madhya Pradesh, besides meeting with the friends and non-Bahá'ís, I attended an educational institute held in a building owned by the Faith and situated in a beautiful and elegant area, formerly the palace of a local governor. There I learned that the believers from all over India came to this institute to deepen themselves in the Bahá'í spiritual and administrative principles, and then returned to their homes to hold similar classes for the youth and children of their communities.

Six Intercontinental Conferences were held in October 1967 in different parts of the world, in honour of the centenary of Bahá'u'lláh's proclamation of His Message to kings and rulers. The Universal House of Justice had opened this celebration by presenting to 140 Heads of State the specially prepared book entitled *The Proclamation of Bahá'u'lláh*. 'The friends', the House of Justice stated in its message to the six Conferences, 'must now take the Message to the rest of humanity.' Six of the Hands of the Cause were appointed to represent the World Centre in these conferences, and I was chosen for the one in Kampala. Before departing for their designated countries, these six Hands met at the World Centre for prayers in the Holy Shrines and then left together by air for Turkey, going on to Edirne (Adrianople) for a day to offer prayers at the House of Bahá'u'lláh where the *Súriy-i-Mulúk* was revealed, and to supplicate Him for confirmation and assistance. Then, with our hearts assured and our spirits rejoiced, we left each other for our separate goals.

The Intercontinental Conference for Africa

The Bahá'í World (vol. XIV, pp. 243–8) has an article about the Kampala Conference; the following excerpts concerning my part in it will be mentioned here, but the reader is urged to turn to the full report in all its fascinating detail.

> . . . The International Conference for Africa was unique in the highlights it produced and the emotions it evoked in the more than four hundred and fifty Bahá'ís from twenty-four nations gathered . . . in Kampala, Uganda . . . Representing the Universal House of Justice, the Hand of the Cause 'Alí-Akbar Furútan read the inspiring message sent from the World Centre to the six Intercontinental Conferences. He spoke of the arduous life of Bahá'u'lláh in Adrianople and the revelation of the *Súriy-i-Mulúk*. He told of the moving experiences of the Hands of the Cause on the pilgrimage to the house of Bahá'u'lláh in Adrianople . . .
>
> On the afternoon of the first day the believers were taken by bus to the Mashriqu'l-Adhkár on Kikaaya Hill where they attended a special service and viewed the portrait of Bahá'u'lláh . . . Following the service, Mr Furútan dedicated the new buildings [of the Ḥaẓíratu'l-Quds of Uganda and Central Africa and a Teaching Institute] designed by Bahá'í architect Patrick Robarts . . .

The Vice-President of India receiving a delegation of Bahá'ís in 1967

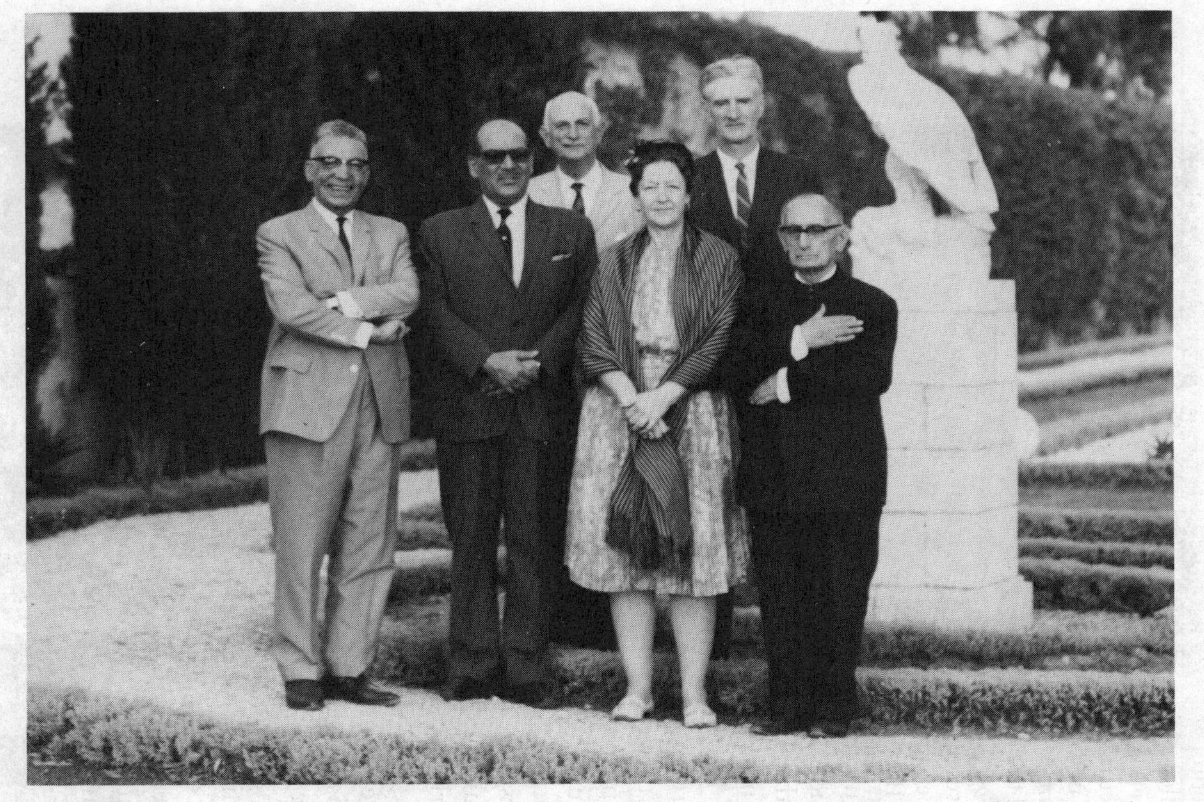

Hands of the Cause of God in the gardens at Bahjí before departing for Edirne and thence to the six Intercontinental Conferences of October 1967

At 5.30 p.m. on the afternoon of the second day a public meeting was held in the main auditorium of Makerere University College. Approximately five hundred people were present to hear Mr Furútan and Mr Olinga speak . . . Following the public meeting a reception for two hundred and fifty people was held at the new State Hotel, attended by representatives of the government, the diplomatic corps, the clergy, educational institutions and the business and professional communities.

. . . [At the last session of the conference] 'Alí-Akbar Furútan, representative of the Universal House of Justice, admonished us to be united and to obey the Law of God if we would win victory for Bahá'u'lláh . . .

Just after the Conference, an opportunity was given for a national television interview about the Faith. The Hand of the Cause Mr Olinga and I spoke in a six-minute programme, and colour pictures of the Shrine of the Báb and the Mashriqu'l-Adhkárs of Kampala and North America were shown on the screen. This interview imparted great joy to the hearts of the believers and apparently was viewed by more than half a million people in Uganda and Kenya. I then visited some of the Bahá'í centres in Uganda, Kenya, Tanzania and Ethiopia, having an interview with the Vice-President of Kenya which lasted over fifty minutes. Before returning to Haifa, more than two weeks were spent in Turkey.

The Centenary of Bahá'u'lláh's Incarceration in the Most Great Prison

The year 1968 was memorable as the centenary of Bahá'u'lláh's voyage from Turkey and His arrival, with His family and some seventy companions, in the prison-city of 'Akká on 31 August 1868. It seemed particularly fitting that this significant milestone in the history of the Faith should be introduced by the convening of the first Bahá'í Oceanic Conference, in Palermo, Sicily, 23–5 August, in the heart of the Mediterranean Sea 'TRAVERSED GOD'S MANIFESTATION

CENTURY AGO' (from cable of the Universal House of Justice, 12 November 1967). It was a prelude to the commemoration at the World Centre of the arrival of Bahá'u'lláh in the Holy Land, to which all participants in the Conference were invited by the Universal House of Justice. More than 2,300 Bahá'ís from 67 countries gathered in Palermo and almost 2,000 of them travelled on to the World Centre. The report of these unforgettable occasions is given in *The Bahá'í World* (vol. XV, pp. 73–86) and it is hoped that my readers will refer to these enlightening and impressive pages and photographs.

Addresses by several Hands of the Cause enriched the Conference programme. At the closing session my own theme was 'Bahá'u'lláh's Ministry in the Holy Land', in which the long history of 'Akká was sketched, as well as its mention in past Holy Books and Bahá'u'lláh's description of it in the *Lawḥ-i-Sulṭán* as 'the most desolate of the cities of the world, the most unsightly of them in appearance, the most detestable in climate, and the foulest in water'. (Cited *God Passes By*, p. 186.)

Here Bahá'u'lláh was condemned to perpetual imprisonment to break His will and end His influence; He responded by renewed proclamation. Here He revealed many of His most important writings including the *Kitáb-i-Aqdas*, and here the flame of His light burned most brightly. Sultan 'Abdu'l-'Azíz is dead and forgotten, while thousands of Bahá'ís have gathered to celebrate the victory of his Victim. 'Chains did not prevent this Cause; imprisonment did not become a barrier . . . From the beginning of the world never before has the Cause of God been proclaimed so openly.' We too must thrive and proclaim in the face of adversity. (I am indebted to the report in *The Bahá'í World* for this summary of my remarks.)

The reply of the Governor of the Province of Palermo to the Italian National Assembly's letter of thanks is worthy of quotation: 'I have been happy to . . . extend hospitality towards the representatives of a spiritual movement of a high moral value and of world-wide importance. I am glad to renew once more to all of you my wishes for the success of your work as I did . . . in the presence of that huge assembly of Bahá'í delegates.' (Translation.)

Soon after the Oceanic Conference, at the request of the Universal House of Justice I returned to Turkey and in about two months visited almost every centre, meeting the National Spiritual Assembly and the Auxiliary Board members, and encouraging unity among the friends.

Another milestone in the onward march of the Faith occurred in June 1968 when the Universal House of Justice announced its 'momentous decision' to establish eleven Continental Boards of Counsellors to ensure the extension into the future of the appointed functions of the institution of the Hands of the Cause of God. Thus the Hands of the Cause gained greater freedom to increase their intercontinental services, while the Universal House of Justice stated its purpose to 'call upon them to undertake special missions on its behalf, to represent it on both Bahá'í and other occasions, and to keep it informed of the welfare of the Cause'. The Hands residing in the Holy Land received the additional responsibilities of serving as liaison between the Universal House of Justice and the Continental Boards, and of assisting in the future establishment of an international teaching centre in the Holy Land, as anticipated by the beloved Guardian. (See *Messages to the Bahá'í World*, pp. 139–44.)

Manifestly, the work and consultations of the Hands residing in the Holy Land increased, while the loving service to the pilgrims continued as before.

World Travels in 1969–1970

The summer of 1969 found me once again undertaking extensive travels in Canada and the United States, as well as

Alaska and Hawaii, before continuing on to the Far East. It is only possible to mention a few of my experiences in North America, from 15 June to 15 September.

During my journey I visited the Mashriqu'l-Adhkár in Wilmette, the Mother Temple of the West and the only one blessed by the presence of 'Abdu'l-Bahá, Who laid its foundation stone in 1912. It is a masterpiece of art and architecture. I also participated in the Bahá'í Schools of Green Acre, Davison (Louhelen), Geyserville and Camp Dorothy Walls, NC, attended many large meetings and fireside gatherings in New York, Dallas, Fort Worth, Memphis, Washington, DC, Columbia (Maryland) and Seattle, and spoke at the National Bahá'í Centre in Wilmette. The number of these meetings was so great that individual description of each is not within the scope of this memoir, and therefore I limit myself to mentioning some of the topics that I talked about in the Bahá'í Schools.

1. I am an Easterner and, according to the customary practices of people, should find myself a stranger among Westerners such as you and be deprived of your friendship. However, as you see, I am neither alone nor abandoned, but am so immersed in the ocean of your kindness and hospitality that I have never missed my own country, and consider you as the members of my family. What other power but the influence of the Teaching of Bahá'u'lláh could foster such unity and brotherhood and eliminate our prejudices? In the Qur'án it is said: '. . . Hadst thou spent all the riches of the earth, thou couldst not have united their hearts; but God hath united them, for He is Mighty, Wise.' (VIII: 64)

In the pages of history unnumbered cruel events and shameful acts of massacre, plunder and repression of the legitimate rights of people have been recorded that bring tears of sorrow to the eyes of every conscious reader. In fact, in the last six thousand years of man's recorded history, it is said, only two hundred years have passed without wars. The rest of the time man, like a ferocious animal, has been engaged in shedding the blood of his own kind. Therefore we, the people of Bahá, should more than ever appreciate this blessed Cause of God, and praise Him for having been born in such a glorious Day, free of our past prejudices.

2. In our age, seven other religions, not counting the Bábí and Bahá'í Faiths, have followers in the world; these are the Sabean religion, Hinduism, Buddhism, Zoroastrianism, Judaism, Christianity and Islam. The only people who profess the truth of all these religions, and recognize their Founders as the true Manifestations of God chosen by Him, are Bahá'ís. This is the exclusive privilege of the followers of Bahá'u'lláh. If others also believed in this blessed Cause and attained this exalted station, all religious prejudices and strife would be eliminated, and man would free himself from the devastating wars which, unfortunately, still continue in our time.

3. The friends are well aware that racial prejudices have for many long years disturbed the peace and tranquillity of mankind, and have stained the earth with the blood of people in different countries. One race says, 'We are white', another, 'We are black', the third, 'We are red', the fourth, 'We are brown', and the fifth asserts that it is yellow. They have fought with each other and destroyed each other's homes only because of difference in the superficial colour of their skins, which is due to nothing but the effect of the rays of the sun.* Even at the present time the flames of this destructive fire have not been extinguished. Blessed are we, the people of Bahá, that we follow this supreme utterance of Bahá'u'lláh: 'O well-beloved ones! The tabernacle of unity hath been raised; regard ye not one another as strangers. Ye

* 'It is the climate of each land which causeth different colours to appear.' ('Abdu'l-Bahá, Maḥmúd's Diary, vol. 2, p. 247.)

are the fruits of one tree, and the leaves of one branch.' (*Tablets of Bahá'u'lláh*, p. 164.)

4. When the Manifestation of God rends the veil of concealment and declares His Mission, He calls all the people of the world, without any exception, to Himself. To every single individual an innate capacity to recognize the Manifestation of the names and attributes of God has been entrusted, and everyone is created with capacity to recognize the Divine Teacher. However, for different reasons people deprive themselves of this heavenly grace and bounty. On this point I would like to recount a story for you. One day in the Western Canada Summer School of British Columbia two individuals approached to bid me farewell. One of these was a Bahá'í, but the other did not consider himself a believer. I asked the non-Bahá'í friend: 'Do you agree that the principles and teachings of the religion of Bahá'u'lláh discussed in the past few days are necessary for the peace and tranquillity of the world?' He replied: 'I cannot deny these principles.' I said: 'Then you are a Bahá'í at heart and, God willing, you will also be a Bahá'í in deeds.' I then gave him this simile, that people are like candles, not like wood or stone. All have the potential to be alight and to enkindle others. Sometimes individuals take a match and light their own candles, but at other times they are neglectful and remain in darkness. I then added that if his Bahá'í friend should light his candle for him, he would be radiant too and would also enkindle others.

One year passed. One day I was waiting for the pilgrims in the Pilgrim House when a young man whose face was familiar arrived. I asked him whether we had met before and he replied: 'I am the same dark candle whom you talked to. I am now enkindled, and have come on pilgrimage on my way to a pioneering post in Africa!'

While in Canada I also had classes at the Laurentian Bahá'í

School, attended the Continental Indian Conference at Fort Qu'Appelle, Saskatchewan, and met Bahá'ís and their guests in St John's, Newfoundland, Vancouver and Saskatoon.

A memorable weekend was spent at the Canadian Atlantic Conference sponsored by the Continental Board of Counsellors for North America – the tenth of a series of deepening conferences – which was held in Halifax, Nova Scotia, 27–9 June. Friends had come from Grand Manan Island, Prince Edward Island and New Brunswick, as well as from Magdalen Islands and Newfoundland where Local Assemblies had been formed for the first time that Riḍván. Consultation was lively and six youth declared their faith in Bahá'u'lláh. The following report of my remarks was published in the US *Bahá'í News* (no. 466, p. 4):

> . . . Mr Furútan spoke of our great bounty and privilege of recognizing the Supreme Manifestation and said that we are too close to the Apostolic Age to realize our bounties. He said that if we hold a book too close to our eyes we cannot read, we must focus to see it. Likewise, we are too close to the age of Bahá'u'lláh to realize His glory and majesty. To be a good Bahá'í, our first duty is to obey Bahá'u'lláh. Our second duty is to teach, to bring the healing Message to the millions of others who have never heard His Name. He said that we Bahá'ís are so few, but the subject is not one of quantity but of quality.* To teach, we should see how 'Abdu'l-Bahá taught. Teach according to the needs and beliefs of the hearers, otherwise it is like a doctor giving a prescription without an examination. Assistance of the Concourse on high, the power that is always in the atmosphere surrounding us, will come through prayers, devotion and the willingness to serve.

* 'Abdu'l-Bahá stated it thus in one of His *Tablets of the Divine Plan* to Canada: 'O ye believers of God! Do ye not look upon the smallness of your number and the multitudes of the nations. Five grains of wheat will be endued with heavenly blessing, whereas a thousand tons of tares will yield no results or effect. One fruitful tree will be conducive to the life of society, whereas a thousand forests of wild trees offer no fruits. The plain is covered with pebbles, but precious stones are rare. One pearl is better than a thousand wildernesses of sand; especially this pearl of great price, which is endowed with divine blessing . . . When that pearl associates and becomes the intimate of the pebbles, they also all change into pearls.'

[He then] brought the final session of the Conference to a beautiful climax . . . Bahá'í conferences are like universities where students come to learn – nobody can claim to understand fully the Bahá'í Writings. Everything is relative and if our capacity at a given time is not fulfilled, the shortcoming is not in the Writings, the shortcoming is in ourselves. Building a new world is making a new race of men. The most difficult thing is to change the minds, habits and hearts of men. This change will come about only through the power of the Manifestation. It is our individual duty to teach the Cause.

I take the liberty of quoting one more report from the Western Canada Summer School because it draws such a happy picture of that delightful place:

Picture if you can Bahá'ís of all ages always on time for classes; eager faces awaiting each word; hearty gales of laughter spreading happiness; bright, friendly eyes spilling love on each other because of the spiritual inspiration . . . walking down the leaf-dappled paths, children holding [his] hand, or sitting on a log by the campfire . . . Imagine how our knowledge and understanding grew . . . (ibid.)

My final meetings with the North American believers were in Alaska at similar deepening conferences held in Juneau and Anchorage in September. Approximately 36 per cent of the Alaskan Bahá'í community attended, 'a very high percentage', in the words of the official report, 'considering the great distances involved, and also considering that this is the period of the year when hunting and fishing activities predominate and last-minute efforts are being made to prepare for the severe winter'. There were representatives of many ethnic groups, including North and Central American Indian, Japanese, Filipino, indigenous Indian tribes of Alaska – Thlingit, Haida, Tsimpsean, Athabascan – Eskimo, Aleut, black and white.

Stopping in Hawaii, where I visited the illumined resting-place of that most peerless of teachers, Miss Martha Root, I had the bounty of visiting the Bahá'ís in six islands and talked on Honolulu television about the Faith. During my next trip to Hawaii, I was happy to meet the Hand of the Cause of God, Agnes Alexander, the veteran pioneer of Japan whom the Master had blessed by His mention of her in *Tablets of the Divine Plan*, and who passed away in Hawaii on 1 January 1971.

I then went on to Japan for the first time. It had been my desire of many years to visit this country, as in my youth I had read a passage by the Master in Maḥmúd's Diary in which He had greatly praised the Japanese, and had bestowed much kindness upon them. I also studied other Tablets of 'Abdu'l-Bahá confirming His praise for Japan, and the following excerpt is from one of these:

> The nation of Japan hath, after a period of decline and impotence, renewed its prime years, hath emerged and is ravishing the hearts of the civilized world in full splendour. Outward appearance reflecteth the inner reality. These material advances are proofs that with the bounty of the Sun of Reality, spiritual progress can be made, and the breath of holiness will soon spread over that land.

The Continental Board of Counsellors in North East Asia was sponsoring a series of deepening conferences, the first being in Tokyo, 18 and 19 October, to be followed by other such conferences in Korea and the Philippine Islands in the first and second weeks of November. Friends from Taiwan, Korea, the Philippine Islands and Guam joined the Japanese believers in Tokyo. A very active schedule of travel and meetings had been arranged for me in Japan and I can mention only several incidents of this eventful trip. There was excellent publicity in the Tokyo *Mainichi Daily News* with a feature article on the Faith. Another public meeting in Iwamizawa impressed itself on my heart because, in addition to the forty-five inquirers, a believer and his family attended who had accepted the Faith three years before during the visit of the Hand of the Cause Mr Samandarí, so recently passed away in Haifa at the close of the centenary commemoration of Bahá'u'lláh's incarceration in the Most Great Prison. Another significant event was a speech I delivered at the University of Osaka on the exalted principles of this holy Cause. This lecture was attended by more than a hundred students and was extremely well received. I also met about twenty-five students at the public meeting in Kyoto. I then attended the Bahá'í Autumn School in Akashi with over fifty believers, while a public meeting there was supported by friends from eleven Japanese cities, and from Taiwan and the Philippine Islands.

Continuing my journey I arrived in Hiroshima, which is now one of the most beautiful cities of Japan with magnificent buildings, wide streets adorned with trees on both sides, and without trace of the destruction it suffered in the Second World War, except for a few ruins kept as a museum. Here we had very fruitful meetings with seekers, thirty-five inquirers at a public meeting remaining for many questions afterwards. There was also a press conference on the teachings of the Faith and my remarks were published in several newspapers in both English and Japanese. One reporter commented that for the first time in that city a speaker, who was a Bahá'í, had considered Buddha to be a Manifestation of God! Hiroshima was the last stop in this Japanese tour. In my meetings with the friends of Tokyo, Osaka, Hiroshima and other cities, I became assured that after rapid expansion of the Cause of God among the people of Japan, the secret of the utterance of 'Abdu'l-Bahá (quoted above) will become clear and manifest to all, and spiritual progress will complement its material advance.

Following these days in Japan, I travelled on to Korea, arriving 31 October for a week's stay. There I met the National Spiritual Assembly and spoke to the Korean

Bahá'ís who had gathered in several deepening conferences.

My next stop was the Philippine Islands, to participate in the two-day Conference, 8 and 9 November, sponsored by the Continental Board of Counsellors. In addition to the seventy-five friends from seventeen communities who attended that weekend, a lively reunion occurred of fourteen Persian student-pioneers from eight universities in six provinces. A 'very high spirit' was generated and it was 'one of the most successful conferences ever held in the Philippines'. At the close of the conference a public meeting attracted forty-five guests of the Bahá'ís.

An unforgettable development was the opportunity to meet eight professors of the Department of Education of the University of the Philippines, by arrangement of one of the student-pioneers, when I spoke openly about the Faith. The result was that they invited me to meet the students and faculty, which I did on 18 November. I was met by the Dean and presented to an audience of about two hundred, and several of the professors invited me to return in future. For that evening the Bahá'ís had arranged a meeting in the College of Agriculture of the same University, and here again at least two hundred faculty members and students were present.

On 23 April 1970 I left the Holy Land to visit European Bahá'í communities for three months that summer. About two months were spent in Germany, first attending the National Convention and later the Bahá'í Summer School in Bremen, with its 150 participants. Their cablegram of 19 July to the World Centre mentioned the 'wonderful spirit' which resulted in two declarations and four pioneer offers. During my stay in Germany I visited most of the Bahá'í communities and took part in two seminars, encountering everywhere the radiant countenances of the friends. There was excellent press coverage during this period and, in fact, the two months from mid-March to mid-May yielded an unprecedented harvest for the German Bahá'í community, with 69 articles in 62 newspapers with a circulation of almost 3.5 million. (I was not the only visitor at that time.) 'Such comprehensive and objective publicity about our beloved Faith is unparalleled in Germany,' was the jubilant summation of the National Assembly. (*Bahá'í International News Service*, no. 29, p. 11.)

In mid-June I went to Austria and, in collaboration with other speakers, contributed to a number of deepening classes in a seminar. I then continued my journey to Denmark, Finland and the Netherlands to teach in their Summer Schools. One of my courses in the Netherlands was especially well received. It was later translated into a number of languages and appeared in the Bahá'í publications of several European countries. It was also published in the form of an essay and has been repeatedly reprinted, even to this day, in India. Following these visits, I returned to the World Centre at the end of July to resume my duties in that sacred land.

13

The Last of the Oceanic Conferences

Between 1968 and 1971 nine Oceanic and Intercontinental Conferences were held. It was my privilege to represent the Universal House of Justice at one of the last two of these, held in Sapporo, Japan, 3–5 September 1971. On the same weekend on the other side of the world the Bahá'ís were also gathered in Reykjavik, Iceland. But before I write of this historic Conference some attention must be given to my journey from Haifa to Japan via the United States, Canada and Alaska where stops were made in the month of August.

The Davison School in Michigan, formerly known as Louhelen and now as I write (1983) resuming this name, was one of the three earliest Summer Schools in the United States, the first being Green Acre, followed by Geyserville and then Louhelen. All three have been thriving Bahá'í Schools for half a century or more, setting a pattern which later Bahá'í Schools have followed, not only in the United States but throughout the world.

I have precious memories of Green Acre and Louhelen which I would like to share. In Green Acre there is a room which was honoured by the footsteps of the beloved Master. When I visited this Summer School, the room was used by the believers for prayers, and every day from dawn until the classes began, a great number of the friends, young and old alike, filled this room to offer most humbly their prayers. Sometimes so many wished to enter that they would have to take their turn and wait in the hall for this precious opportunity. I found at the Davison School in 1971 that a room had also been set aside for dawn prayers. To me these were evidences of the transforming power of the Cause of God. Otherwise, Westerners, who are generally unfamiliar with the concept of dawn prayers, would never have chosen to leave their couches in the early hours of dawn to engage in the remembrance of God.

On my way to Alaska I attended the National Conference of Bahá'ís of Canada held in Halifax, Nova Scotia, where I had been in 1969, as mentioned in earlier pages.

My schedule in Alaska was to attend a Summer School in Juneau from 22 to 25 August, then travel north to Anchorage for a Deepening Conference on 28–29 August. It was my second visit to Alaska, which had at that time received in years past the visits of eight other Hands of the Cause of God.

There was an amusing incident in Juneau at the time of my arrival which I have never forgotten. One of the American friends and I had been invited to teach at the Summer School and we planned to stay at the same hotel. As she had the names of our Bahá'í contacts in Juneau I did not trouble to note the addresses and telephone numbers myself. However, on the way to the hotel she decided to go to another hotel. I spent the night and in the morning, on looking at the school programme, found that I was to open the school at 9.30 a.m. but I had no way of finding the school or of contacting any of the Bahá'ís! I went to the lobby and anxiously waited for help. There was a German Shepherd dog lying in the lobby and I amused myself by watching him. Just then a little girl of six or seven came into the lobby, went straight to the dog and began playing with him. It was evident that they knew each other. After she had played with the dog for a time, she looked at me and with surprise and joy asked me if I was Mr Furútan! I was more surprised than she and replied, 'How do you know me?' 'Oh,' she said, 'my mother has brought your picture from the Holy Land and has shown it to us.' Excitedly I asked whether she knew where the Summer School was, and she said that she and her parents had come from another town for the school and she would take me there. It was as if I had been given all the treasures of the world! She held my arm and took me straight to the school, which was in fact very close to the hotel. We arrived exactly at 9.30 and my punctuality was greatly admired by the school administrators! Later on, I corresponded with my dear little friend; she always signed her letters 'your dog-lover friend'!

The *Alaska Bahá'í News* for October 1971 devoted nearly six pages to descriptions of the two events in Juneau and Anchorage and I can only choose a small amount of this lavish coverage for my memoir. According to this report I spoke briefly on six subjects: Teaching, The Unity of Mankind, The Trinity, The Son of God, Miracles, and The Institution of the Hands and the Continental Boards of Counsellors. On the last evening some of my own experiences with the beloved Guardian were shared. 'All these sessions', according to the report, 'were seasoned with . . . humour and story-telling . . . He says that he tries always to make people happy, as 'Abdu'l-Bahá said we should, and he certainly succeeded during these sessions.'

For the Deepening School in Anchorage there were many Bahá'ís, not only from the Anchorage area but from Fairbanks, Kodiak, Unalaska and other far-away places. My themes were The Real Meaning of Independent Investigation of Truth, True Liberty in the Cause of Bahá'u'lláh, Building a New World, and All Things Made New. Using quotations from the Writings and referring the friends to others, I reminded the believers, among many other points, that there are only two kinds of freedom for Bahá'ís: to follow the Laws of God as revealed by Bahá'u'lláh ('True liberty consisteth in man's submission unto My commandments', *Gleanings*, CLIX), and to be free from all material attachments. A question was asked about taking children from settled to rural areas where school facilities are limited. I replied that if pioneers go to such rural areas the schools may be poor but the 'education' good. You should 'listen to the voice of your heart . . . Our first obligation is to teach . . . and the second, to educate our children according to Bahá'í Teachings.' The official report, I noted, was a useful source of humorous stories, should I ever need them in future!

Leaving Alaska with praise for this energetic and successful Bahá'í community, I departed for Japan and the historic Oceanic Conference in the island of Hokkaido in its far north. Hokkaido is the home of the Ainu, the aboriginal people of Japan whose racial characteristics differ from the majority of the Japanese population. I arrived at Osaka and from there, in the company of a few believers, flew on to Sapporo, the capital of Hokkaido. During the drive from the airport we saw, to our joy, white banners on both sides of the road bearing the Greatest Name. This idea appealed to Bahá'ís and non-Bahá'ís so much that it is hard to describe it. Also, as we passed through the streets of Sapporo, we saw many posters on the walls and in the windows of various shops announcing the Conference and its public meeting. I learned later that the dear friends had obtained excellent publicity, with two thousand posters and fifty thousand pamphlets being distributed, and that in one month of intensive teaching just prior to the Conference there were 150 declarations in Hokkaido. Moreover, there were two television appearances and three radio programmes dealing with the Conference, and numerous articles in both English and Japanese language newspapers.

The statistics of the Conference are impressive. Besides myself, as representative of the Universal House of Justice, there were two other Hands of the Cause of God, Mr Collis Featherstone and Dr Raḥmatu'lláh Muhájir, six

Scandinavian Bahá'í Summer School near Aarhus, Jutland, Denmark, 5–12 July 1970

バハイ北太平洋会議・札幌・1971

BAHA'I NORTH PACIFIC OCEANIC CONFERENCE ·SAPPORO·1971

Counsellors, eleven Auxiliary Board members, representatives of National Spiritual Assemblies, and a total of 625 Bahá'ís from 31 countries and territories. For many believers, especially from small islands in the Pacific and villages in Hokkaido, it was their first opportunity to meet Bahá'ís from all over the world and experience the unity of their Faith.

The message from the Universal House of Justice reminded the Conference that Hokkaido 'first heard of the Teachings less than fifteen years ago, and the first aboriginal peoples of this land accepted Bahá'u'lláh just over a decade ago . . . We are heartened at the prospect that from the indigenous peoples of this vast oceanic area, the Ainu, the Japanese, the Chinese, the Koreans, the Okinawans, the Micronesians, the American Indians, the Eskimos, and the Aleuts vast numbers will soon enter the Faith . . . The sweet perfume of victory is in the air, and we must hasten to achieve it while there is yet time.' (*The Bahá'í World*, vol. XV, pp. 321–2.)

One of the significant events of this Conference was the public proclamation meeting. The National Spiritual Assembly of Japan had invited two prominent scholars of Japan to speak: Dr Kuniyoshi Obara, President of Tamagawa University in Tokyo, and Dr Harusada Suginome, Chairman, Commission for UNESCO in Hokkaido and former president of the Island's university. Our talks were about education, one from the Bahá'í standpoint (translated into Japanese). Not a seat was empty and many had to stand throughout the meeting. Of the audience of six hundred, 150 were inquirers of Buddhist and Christian background, including some Christian nuns in their habits. At the end of the meeting, twenty-three declared their Faith in Bahá'u'lláh, and many others asked for Bahá'í literature. (During the Conference there were thirty-six declarations and another seventy in the four days of intensive teaching following the Conference.) The two Japanese speakers later expressed their admiration for the Teachings and Dr Obara presented me with several of his books in both English and Japanese. I heard also that he had spoken about the Teachings of the Faith for almost half an hour, praising its principles and laws during a television programme designed to introduce the Faith to the public on 19 September. This programme had a tremendous impact on the expansion of the faith in that country.

The tangible results of this historic Conference were as follows:

1. More than $80,000 was pledged for the goals of the Nine Year Plan.
2. Twenty-one believers volunteered to travel and teach.
3. A delegation consisting of the Hand of the Cause Collis Featherstone and myself, with several other well-known Bahá'ís, presented to the Governor of Hokkaido, Mr Naohiro Dogakinai, a copy of *The Proclamation of Bahá'u'lláh*. A photograph of the presentation ceremony was published in some of the newspapers of Sapporo.

Post-Conference Travels

Soon after the Oceanic Conference I went again to Hiroshima where I had been in October 1969. There I addressed a public meeting with an unprecedented number of inquirers present, their response to the message of the Faith being most enthusiastic. Next I went to Kobe and spoke to another large group of non-Bahá'ís. Ten university students who were present accepted Bahá'u'lláh. Such response prompted me to comment on the hopefulness of the Faith's progress in Japan, for in the past the friends were happy with a few declarations in a year.

A Post-Oceanic Conference was being held in Manila, 17–19 September, and I travelled on to the Philippine Islands to attend it. There I found Bahá'ís from Iran, the United States, Alaska, thirty Philippine communities and four other countries 'met together in the glowing spirit of a true Bahá'í family'. News of the passing of the Hand of the Cause of God Músá Banání reached us, and in paying tribute to this precious friend I said that 'everyone is living temporarily in this world and that we all desire a good ending, that is, to go to the Abhá Kingdom serving the Cause with full hands. Mr Banání was such an example.'

On the last evening a public proclamation programme was held at the National Press Club, attended by over four hundred persons. Several declarations included two professors from the University of the Philippines; much to my joy one greeted me with 'Alláh-u-Abhá'! Dr Muhájir and I also met more than 250 students and teachers in an exclusive high school, the UP Preparatory School. The report of my remarks on this occasion states:

> . . . a psychologist and child educator, he swept the whole audience with his infectious humour. Gearing the universal theme of Bahá'u'lláh's teaching to his youthful audience, he fired their enthusiasm and curiosity by his very scientific explanation of Bahá'u'lláh's principles.

Once more it was my privilege to see the dear friends in Australia and New Zealand. Travelling to different Australian cities, I talked with a great number of believers and seekers, and was interviewed several times by reporters. Then, from 7 to 11 October I was in Auckland, having stopped briefly in Christchurch. Here I spoke on science and religion, apparently in a 'highly entertaining' way, to about a hundred people, mainly Bahá'ís, and again to sixty Bahá'ís on the Institution of the Hands of the Cause of God. When asked for a deepening session in Australia, I reminded the friends that more of the Writings of Bahá'u'lláh and more books on the Faith have been published in English than in any other Western language, and that deepening is a matter of allotting the time to read the storehouse of literature available.

Before leaving this account of my services in 1971, I should like to share one of my memories of Australia. One day I met a Protestant minister, a radiant and dignified gentleman but fanatical in his religious beliefs. We discussed several subjects, and finally the prophecies of the Bible concerning the return of Christ. As expected, he gave a literal interpretation to all these prophecies, anticipating that Christ will appear from the sky, the stars will fall and the earth will shake, etc. Unable to persuade him to consider other interpretations, I decided to ask him a question and said: 'In the first chapter of Genesis God has revealed: ". . . Let there be light: and there was light. And God saw the light, that it was good; and God divided the light from darkness. And God called the light Day, and the darkness he called Night. And the evening and the morning were the first day . . . And God said, Let there be lights in the firmament of the heaven to divide the day from the night; . . . And God made two great lights; the greater light to rule the day, and the lesser light to rule the night: he made the stars also . . . And the evening and the morning were the fourth day."' (1:3–19) I then asked him, 'If God created the sun, moon and stars, which are the source of light, only on the fourth day, then what was the meaning of morning and evening on the previous days? And how did light exist without the sun, moon, and stars?' (I had read this explanation by 'Abdu'l-Bahá in Maḥmúd's Diary.*) The old man looked at me in astonishment and said sincerely: 'I have read these verses many times, but had not noticed this point. You are right. There is an ambiguity in these verses!'

* 'What is intended by the creation of heaven and earth in six days is a spiritual creation and a divine day, as prior to the creation of this heaven and earth there were no days and nights.' (vol. 1, p. 403.)

I then simply added that therefore one should consider the allusions in the Bible as spiritual mysteries, and not interpret them in literal terms. The return of Christ should be understood in this way.

14

The Close of the Nine Year Plan

During the final year of the Nine Year Plan I was privileged to visit six countries in Asia and Europe, in two separate journeys from the World Centre, the first at Riḍván 1972, primarily to represent the Universal House of Justice at the historic first National Convention of the Bahá'ís of Nepal, stopping also in India and briefly in Turkey as I returned; the second in the late summer and winter of 1972–3 when my trip included Turkey, Switzerland, Germany and Norway. The purpose of this second journey was to aid and encourage the friends in their strenuous efforts to achieve their goals in those closing months of the Plan.

I shall also include in this chapter the travels I undertook between 8 August and 24 October 1973, when consolidation of the goals won and deepening of the believers were of first importance.

First National Convention of Nepal

Nepal is situated just above the north-eastern frontier of India, lying entirely within the great ranges of the Himalayas except for a narrow strip on its southern border. Many of the world's highest mountains stand in Nepal, including Mt Everest. The kingdom's area is 141,414 sq. km. and its population in 1978 was 13,421,000.

Leaving Haifa on 16 April 1972, my first stop was in New Delhi for a few days with the Bahá'ís, especially the youth, and I shared the first day of Riḍván with them. I then boarded a small plane of the Nepal airline, in the company of two other believers, for our flight to Katmandu, the

The first National Convention of the Bahá'ís of Nepal, Katmandu, Riḍván 1972

Delegates attending the first National Convention in Nepal, Riḍván 1972

The first National Spiritual Assembly of the Bahá'ís of Nepal

capital of Nepal. While flying over the unattainable snow-covered mountains of the Himalayas, our small plane jerked and jolted until we finally reached Katmandu! The city itself appeared to resemble other cities of the Indian sub-continent, but should the Bahá'í traveller go into the countryside he would rejoice greatly in the refreshing air and surroundings, and would recall these words of Bahá'u'lláh: 'The country is the world of the soul, the city is the world of bodies.' (Esslemont, *Bahá'u'lláh and the New Era*, p. 48.) The people of Katmandu are most friendly and hospitable and easily attract visitors to themselves.

During my stay we saw a number of Western youth who lived there content although in utmost poverty. I heard that their dwelling was a half-destroyed room where they spent the severely cold nights of winter. One day, when visiting with another friend a famous Buddhist temple on the top of a mountain overlooking Tibet, I saw another group of these youth sitting around the temple, obviously with nothing to do. I was so grieved at this sight and remarked to my Bahá'í friends, 'I wish that the Bahá'ís of this city, in consultation with the Spiritual Assembly, would take some measures to speak to these youth about the Cause of God. Perhaps the hearts of some of them would be illumined by its light.'

The first National Convention of the Bahá'ís of Nepal was attended by the national delegates, the representative of the National Spiritual Assembly of India, and a number of Counsellors and members of Auxiliary Boards. The Convention was convened by prayers read in the Nepalese, Arabic, Persian, English and Indian languages, after which the message from the Universal House of Justice was read. 'The believers who had gathered in Katmandu . . . were moved to tears of thanksgiving as they heard the words they had laboured so arduously to earn.' Throughout the Convention each one of the participants, who were from different religious backgrounds, manifested true spirituality and radiance. The delegates discharged their duties in utmost order, according to the scheduled programme, and after full consideration elected the members of their first National Spiritual Assembly. (See *The Bahá'í World*, vol. XV, p. 249.)

On the initiative of this newly elected Assembly, each night a number of Government authorities and notables of the city were invited to dinner in a hotel. During the course of conversation, the teachings and principles of the Faith were discussed, and thus several dignitaries, university professors, authors and newspaper editors became familiar with the Cause of God. Among them were a few who had been in Haifa and had seen and admired the sacred Shrines. The director of the University library invited me to visit his library where I was most respectfully received.

During these days much time was given to assisting the beloved members of the National Spiritual Assembly, since many of them had never before served on an Assembly. There was also a Deepening Conference following the Convention, after which reluctant farewells were said and I resumed my travels, going back to India for its National Convention in Poona.

Following the Convention it was my joy to attend the lively Fourth Annual Youth Convention in Poona, attended by forty-three representatives from twenty-six local Youth Committees from all over India, as well as some fifty observers. A cable sent to the Universal House of Justice on 8 May pledged a number of achievements for the final year of the Nine Year Plan from this gathering of youth who were 'THRILLED OPPORTUNITY RESPOND CALL SUPREME BODY . . . ' Publicity for this event was excellent and included considerable quotation of my remarks in the newspapers of Poona.

I returned to the World Centre via Turkey to visit some of the believers there. The same summer, August 1972, I returned to Turkey to meet the Bahá'í community of Istanbul and consult with the National Spiritual Assembly.

Two Tours in Europe

This second visit to Turkey began a tour to three countries of Europe – Switzerland, Germany and Norway – which was followed a year later, August 1973, by a more extended tour to eight countries.

My first stop in 1972, after Turkey, was in Switzerland where I met the National Spiritual Assembly and also participated in meetings in Nyon, Vevey, Neuchâtel, Basel and Wolfhalden, where a Bahá'í Exposition was held. Among those present at Wolfhalden was one of the first Swiss Bahá'ís, and there were also many new believers.

Going on to Germany, I visited many Bahá'í communities, 'travelling almost without pause to urge . . . the friends . . . to sacrifice for the victorious termination of the Nine Year Plan. In Ludwigsburg, accompanied by the Chairman of the Assembly and Mrs Grossmann,' I met the Lord Mayor of the city and presented a copy of *The Proclamation of Bahá'u'lláh*.

Then on to Norway where I was much impressed by the many newly-enlisted youth. In Bærum, near Oslo, the enthusiasm of a High School audience kept me answering their questions for two hours. Here and in Bodø which I visited, lying north of the Arctic Circle, new Local Assemblies were formed at Riḍván 1973. Trondheim was another city included in this tour.

During the summer of 1973, soon after the conclusion of the Nine Year Plan, it was my bounty to see many of my European Bahá'í friends again and to encourage them in consolidating their victories during that Plan. Leaving Haifa on 18 August, I went first to Paris for two large meetings, as well as one with travelling teachers and youth who had come from the United States. All were a source of joy, as was my visit to Madame Dreyfus-Barney who, although over ninety years of age, vividly recalled her times with ‘Abdu’l-Bahá when, in the course of several extended visits to the Holy Land from the beginning of this century until 1908, she recorded the Master’s answers to her wide-ranging questions, resulting in one of our most important books, *Some Answered Questions*. (See Balyuzi, *‘Abdu’l-Bahá*, pp. 81–2.) After Paris I went south to the French Summer School, held in a beautiful region near Marseilles. Over two hundred believers from fifteen countries of both East and West attended. ‘An exciting characteristic of this school was the participation of many new, young, enthusiastic French Bahá’ís whose presence promised much hope for the future of their country,’ and these I encouraged to ‘take the lead in Bahá’í activities’. Truly, the spiritual and physical character of that School was so outstanding that it cannot be put into words.

After visiting the friends in Orleans, on 3 September I arrived in Lisbon for my travels in Portugal, a significant part of this tour. In Faro, in the extreme south, it was an inspiring experience ‘to see the number of Portuguese believers who were ablaze with the fire of the love of God’; a Bahá’í couple who pioneered there from Latin America had much to do with this, but I was impressed also by the lady in whose home a meeting was held and whose five children were imbued with the spirit of the Cause although their father was not a believer, as well as by a most promising Bahá’í youth of Faro. Still in the south, I stopped in Portimão, then went north to Setúbal, Coimbra and Porto, everywhere meeting the pioneers, their families and friends in gatherings often lasting until midnight. I arrived in Lisbon on 8 September, participated in a youth gathering and spent the whole of the next day with thirty or forty believers from Portugal, America and Iran who had gathered at the site of the future Mas͟hriqu'l-Ad͟hkár, a 'beautiful spot looking out to the Atlantic Ocean'.

Leaving Portugal on 10 September I flew to Madrid for a week in Spain and was made happy by the sincerity and spirituality of the Bahá'ís. I shall never forget meeting over two hundred friends in the Bahá'í Centre of a small village.

As my tour included participation in the Italian Summer School I flew to Rome on 17 September. The School was attended by over three hundred, and I was scheduled to teach each morning and evening. Here is a summary of one of my talks:

'The scholars and scientists of the world have laboured for years to discover the mysteries of nature. The sheer volume and, in particular, the results of their researches are truly astonishing. For example, they have discovered that electrons spin around the nuclei of their atoms about 1,000 billion times per second! Or, the continent of America advances 20 cm. per year towards the West, while the continents of Europe and Asia advance towards the East with the same speed, and in 4 million years, America will connect with Asia from the West. They have also found that the human brain has 10 billion cells; lungs weigh 1200 gr. in males and 900 gr. in females; the total length of all the veins of the human body is 650,000 km.; 700,000 different species of vegetation grow on the earth, and each one has been given a name; the sun synthesizes 400 billion tons of hydrogen every 24 hours to produce helium, and will continue to do so for another 10 billion years; there are approximately 50,000 strands of hair on the head of each male and 70,000 on the head of each female; and so forth.

'Now if the scholars and learned of the world had pursued the mysteries of the realm of truth and spirit with the same vigour and patience, and had investigated, discussed and studied the teachings of Bahá'u'lláh, which are the only means for the redemption of mankind from its ignorant prejudices causing so many useless wars, the face of the earth would not have been so savagely stained with the blood of its peoples, and wars and contention would have been transformed into peace and tranquillity.

'If cities are to be bombarded with atom bombs and destroyed in a matter of seconds, what benefit is gained from the discovery of the speed of electrons? When thousands upon thousands of people and millions of soldiers lose their lives or their limbs in wars, what is the use of knowing how many strands of hair a man or a woman has? And when miles and miles of farms, meadows and forests are burned to ashes in the twinkling of an eye, what is the advantage in knowing the names of species of vegetation?

'The ultimate purpose of all the discoveries and inventions, and all the labour that is expended in scientific fields should be to secure the peace and tranquillity of mankind. If knowledge and science result in humanity's desolation and in the destruction of cities and countries, then they have failed in their supreme purpose; in other words, the remedy has added to the disease.

'For this reason, Bahá'u'lláh in numerous Tablets has called the people of the world to unity and concord and to the elimination of their prejudices. The following are extracts from His Writings:

'The aim of this Wronged One in sustaining woes and tribulations, in revealing the Holy Verses and in demonstrating proofs hath been naught but to quench the flame of hate and enmity, that the horizon of the hearts of men may be illumined with the light of concord and attain real peace and tranquillity. (*Tablets of Bahá'u'lláh*, p. 219)

'It behoveth man to adhere tenaciously unto that which will promote fellowship, kindliness and unity. (ibid., p. 90)

'O contending peoples and kindreds of the earth! Set your faces towards unity, and let the radiance of its light shine upon you. (*Gleanings*, CXI.)

'It is binding and incumbent upon the peoples of the world, one and all, to extend aid unto this momentous Cause which is come from the heaven of the Will of the ever-abiding God, that perchance the fire of animosity which blazeth in the hearts of some peoples of the earth may, through the living waters of divine wisdom and by virtue of heavenly counsels and exhortations, be quenched, and the light of unity and concord may shine forth and shed its radiance upon the world. (*Tablets of Bahá'u'lláh*, p. 23.)

"Abdu'l-Bahá has also uttered these words on this subject:

'The wild beast hunts at most once a day for its food, but cruel man slays a hundred thousand people each day for fame and power. If a lamb is rent asunder by a wolf, the wolf is killed, but if a man moistens the earth with the blood of a hundred thousand people, he is called a general or a marshal, and is honoured and respected. If a human being kills another human being, or sets a home afire, he is called a murderer and a criminal, but if he destroys a camp, or devastates a country he is called a conqueror and is idolized. If someone steals one dollar, he is imprisoned, but if he plunders the homes of the people, and loots a city, he is called a commander and is praised. (Maḥmúd's Diary, vol. 1, p. 287.)

'As long as these prejudices prevail, the world of humanity will not have rest . . . all mankind are of one nation . . . all the world is man's birthplace . . . In the creation . . . boundaries and outlets were not assigned. (*Selections*, pp. 299–300.)'

There followed a busy and fruitful fortnight in Germany with special deepening conferences, particularly attracting the Bahá'í youth. These were held in four regions – Cologne, Langenhain, Ulm and Esslingen-Stuttgart, with large attendances nearly everywhere; there were over three hundred in each of the first two regions mentioned. In many of these classes the believers asked for a detailed explanation of the *Kitáb-i-Aqdas*. In general, I reminded the students that, in order to appreciate the revealed verses of the Mother Book of the Bahá'í Dispensation, one must acquaint oneself, at least briefly, with the Holy Books of previous religions, and try to comprehend the wisdom of the heavenly teachings and laws revealed in each of these Books. One cannot gain a sufficient understanding of Bahá'í Holy Writings without such knowledge. It was also explained that comprehension of the terms used in the Holy Books facilitates the process of learning; for example, if Buddhists or Hindus or Zoroastrians should wish to study the New Testament, they would need to acquaint themselves with such expressions as Pharisees, Scribes, Sadducees, Adam, Eve, Heavenly Father, Sons of God, Kingdom of Heaven and others, to understand the real meaning of the utterances of Christ.

References to several Holy Books were offered for individual deepening, as follows:

Old Testament	Leviticus, chapters 11, 17 to 21
	Exodus, chapters 21 to 23
New Testament	Matthew 5:17–20
	Luke 16:17
	Acts 24:14
Qur'án	Sura IV (Women)
Bahá'u'lláh's Tablets	Ishráqát, Bishárát, Ṭarázát, Tajallíyát, Kalimát-i-Firdawsíyyih, all of which supplement the most Holy Book, and Lawḥ-i-Dunyá and Lawḥ-i-Maqṣúd. (See *Tablets of Bahá'u'lláh*.)

A summary of these lectures was published in *Bahá'í-Nachrichten*, the Bahá'í News of Germany.

Bahá'í Summer School in Carry-le-Rouet, France, August 1973

A Deepening Conference in Cologne (Köln), Germany, October 1973

During this fortnight I also met the friends of Luxemburg in two meetings whose sweetness I shall never forget. Then came a week in Austria beginning 15 October, when I visited the believers in Vienna, Graz, and Linz, also attending a conference for the Austrian Bahá'ís. My feelings and impressions of this gathering, so spiritual and enthusiastic, I am unable to record.

At the conclusion of these truly unforgettable months, I returned to the Holy Land via Athens and, after a few days there, arrived in Israel on 26 October.

15

Services in the Five Year Plan: 1974–1979

At Riḍván 1974 the Universal House of Justice inaugurated 'the third global plan embarked upon by the Army of Light in its implementation of 'Abdu'l-Bahá's Divine Plan . . .' in a message which galvanized the Bahá'í world community. 'A span of eighteen years separates us from the centenary of Bahá'u'lláh's Ascension and the unveiling of His Almighty Covenant. The fortunes of humanity in that period no man can foretell . . . Undismayed and undeterred by the wreckage of "long-cherished ideals and time-honoured institutions", . . . the world community of Bahá'ís must surge forward eagerly, and with ever-increasing energy, to build those new, God-given institutions from which will be diffused the light of the holy principles and teachings sent down by God in this day for the salvation of all mankind.'

Already in the Holy Land, on 5 June 1973, the Universal House of Justice had brought into being the International Teaching Centre, consisting of all the Hands of the Cause of God together with three Counsellor members* who had been serving in South America, North America and Africa. It was a development, wrote the Universal House of Justice three days later, 'which, at one and the same time, brings to fruition the work of the Hands of the Cause residing in the Holy Land and provides for its extension into the future, links the institution of the Boards of Counsellors even more intimately with that of the Hands of the Cause of God, and powerfully reinforces the discharge of the rapidly growing

* A fourth was appointed from Europe in 1979.

responsibilities of the Universal House of Justice'. One of the first tasks assigned to the International Teaching Centre was 'to devise the broad outlines of the global teaching plan to begin at Riḍván 1974 and conclude five years later at Riḍvan 1979'. (See *The Bahá'í World*, vol. XVII, pp. 324–5.) At this time the world community had grown from twelve National Spiritual Assemblies in 1953, at the start of the World Crusade (the first global teaching plan) to 113, with 17,000 Local Assemblies and 69,500 centres. On the other hand, the number of the Hands of the Cause of God, described by the Universal House of Justice as 'one of the most precious assets the Bahá'í world possesses', and the Faith's 'ambassadors-at-large', had decreased from twenty-seven at the time of the beloved Guardian's passing in 1957 to sixteen for the work of the Five Year Plan. The reader will appreciate, therefore, that my own humble services to this Plan, by the instructions of the Universal House of Justice, could only increase in the field of travel to many countries throughout the world. For this final chapter of my memoirs I have decided to summarize these journeys under the headings of the three continents, Asia, Europe and North America, which I visited and revisited in these five years.

A. ASIA

Iran

In March 1974 the Universal House of Justice decided that I should again visit Iran after seven years (my last visit was in 1966), to represent the World Centre in the National Convention of that country. The Five Year Plan was announced to the Bahá'í world in that year, and the compatriots of the Greatest Name were to be encouraged to take the lead, with the grace and bounty of God, in the fields of teaching and pioneering. The accounts of this journey are recorded in detail in the letters of the National Spiritual

Assembly of Iran and the Local Spiritual Assembly of Tehran, addressed to the World Centre, and may be summarized as follows:

In Tehran three to four meetings were held every day, each lasting for one-and-a-half hours, and each attended by more than 300 believers.

This series of meetings continued for four months.

Deepening classes were held for youth three days a week. These classes continued for a month and were attended by a total of 800 youth.

Junior youth classes were held every morning for one week, with an attendance of 150 each day.

A special one-week course was held for 250 teachers of the Bahá'í classes.

Special classes for Bahá'í women were held every day for two weeks, with more than 400 attending each class.

A few meetings were held for the graduates of institutions of higher learning, each attended by 200 believers.

In the Summer School near Tehran, which lasted for forty days and was attended by a total of 2,500 believers, seventy hours of lectures were given.

In addition to the National Convention of the Bahá'ís of Iran, meetings were consecutively held at the Summer School with the National Convention of Bahá'í Women, the National Youth Convention, and a large gathering of teachers of Bahá'í classes from various parts of Iran.

This servant also attended numerous consultative meetings of the Hands of the Cause of God, the Counsellors, and members of the Auxiliary Boards.

Twelve hundred Bahá'í children were met in one gathering.

For two months individual Bahá'ís were met privately.

These consultations were later reduced to three times a week, and then weekly.

Unnumbered gatherings were arranged in seven other cities that I might meet the believers and convey to them news of the Bahá'í world.

Pilgrimages to the Bahá'í Holy Places in Iran were also my privilege during this journey.

Three years later I spent another four months in Iran, having come from Japan on 10 October 1977, and carried out another programme of intensive teaching until I returned to the Holy Land.

Conferences with Persian Bahá'ís in Germany and England in 1977 will be mentioned below.

Turkey

It was three years since my last brief visit to Turkey and so it brought happiness both to me and the dear Turkish friends to be with them in 1975 during September and part of October. There were meetings both day and night in Istanbul, Ankara, Izmir, Bursa, Bornova, Kúchik-Chakmachih and other centres, attended by local believers who, despite transportation difficulties, managed to come from outlying areas. The following encouraging words were written by the National Spiritual Assembly of that country: 'The friends were delighted . . . one could see great joy and happiness in their faces and feel the power of love . . . showered upon them. The youth were very eager to learn – they would come with their note pads and take notes for later reference.'

India

The Republic of India, a sub-continent which extends from the mountain ranges of the Himalayas to the Indian Ocean, is the seventh largest country in the world, its 700 millions representing a richly-varied range of peoples of many national and religious backgrounds, of whom 82 per cent are Hindus.

The name of India entered Bahá'í history in the time of the Báb in the person of Shaykh Sa'íd-i-Hindí, an early disciple and Letter of the Living, himself an Indian who died in his native land in unknown circumstances. There is also record of an Indian navváb who, following a vision of the Báb, made his way on foot to Chihríq to meet his 'heart's desire' and received from Him a new name. (See *The Dawn-Breakers*, p. 304, and Balyuzi's *The Báb*, p. 137.)

During the ministry of Bahá'u'lláh, many of the well-known teachers of the Faith travelled to India and taught the Faith there. Later, the marble sarcophagus, to which the sacred remains of the Báb were transferred for final interment, was made in Burma, then closely associated with India. Many of the Afnáns have had commercial dealings with India, and served as points of contact between the Bahá'ís of India and Iran.

The Master, 'Abdu'l-Bahá, has bestowed great bounties upon India in His numerous Tablets, and the following excerpts are examples of His utterances:

> It is the wish of my heart and soul that the Sun of the divine heavens will shine with such splendour and beauty in that country that India will become a rose garden . . . India will sweeten the palates with delectable sweetness, will mingle ambergris and musk, and mix milk with honey. (*To the Bahá'ís of Mandalay.*)

> That country will ultimately be illumined and that land will become the paradise of delight. (*To Jináb-i-Maḥmúd Zarqání.*)

> 'Abdu'l-Bahá deeply longeth to travel to India, if conditions and circumstances permit. (ibid.)

The beloved Guardian in a letter to the Bahá'ís of Iran and India, March 1922, states:

India, whether by virtue of its size and the ancient history of its civilization, or the diversity of its beliefs, religions and races, and the receptivity of its inhabitants, is a ripe and vast field for the diffusion of the Word of God and the hoisting of the banner of His Religion. Particularly, it was, in the latter years of the Centre of the Covenant, the recipient of His special favours and derived joy and hope from His divine promises.

On 2 November 1976, I left Haifa for India and was there until the 20th. My first meeting was with the beloved friends and pioneers of New Delhi, after which I attended a four-day conference of the Counsellors, Auxiliary Board members, and members of the National Spiritual Assemblies of India, Bangladesh and Sikkim. During this time, accompanied by a representative of the National Spiritual Assembly of India, I met the Deputy Vice-President of India, three Government Ministers of Housing and Development, Information and the Interior, and the Speaker of the Parliament, discussing the tenets of the Faith in detail with each of them.

A magnificent Conference in Gwalior, which I attended on 11 November, was held in the former palace of the Maharajah, one of the most beautiful buildings of that area. Meeting under very attractive and colourful pavilions, more than a thousand believers, mostly native to India, consulted about the objectives of the Five Year Plan. The first session was convened by the Governor of Madhya Pradesh, who brought with him thirty other dignitaries of the State. The Governor, in his lengthy talk, praised the teachings of the Faith, and I also spoke in detail in that session. There followed many Bahá'í songs in different languages. The entire session was broadcast on radio in English and Hindi, by instruction of the Governor. Since there was not enough space for a group photograph near the pavilions, a Bahá'í lady who was Professor of Anatomy in the University of Gwalior, obtained permission for this to be made in the university precincts. As the thousand believers walked through the winding streets to the university, many curious bystanders watched in amazement as we passed. The photographer who had taken the official pictures of the 1953 Intercontinental Teaching Conference in New Delhi was invited to come to Gwalior and again proved his skill. The President, Deans of several Faculties, and students of the University cheerfully welcomed us and provided all necessary facilities.

After the successful conclusion of the conference, I visited the friends of Bombay in the company of a few believers and then went on to Poona for a similar meeting, after which we continued our tour to Panchgani.

A Bahá'í primary and secondary school has existed in Panchgani for a number of years, adding to its prestige and development every year. It is now one of the outstanding Bahá'í educational institutions and, at the time of my visit, had five hundred students. Half the students were Bahá'ís and the rest non-Bahá'ís from various parts of India and other countries of the world. We were welcomed by the principal, teachers, and all the students with a beautiful programme and in the next two days were able to become acquainted with the teachers and students, and also lecture on education several times. We stayed for two nights in a fine building just purchased for the expansion of the school into a college. From the balcony we overlooked a beautiful landscape of mountains, valley and river, all a delight to the eyes. It is not in vain that Panchgani has been called the Switzerland of that region. The local Ḥaẓíratu'l-Quds stood in a similarly pleasant area, and here one could immerse oneself in meditation and feel much closer to God in that attractive environment.

After this delightful stay we returned to Poona to meet the friends once again before leaving for Bombay to take our flight to Hong Kong for the Bahá'í International

Teaching Conference.

At this point I would like to refer my readers to Appendix 1 for a brief summary of my speeches in India which includes a number of relevant passages from Bahá'í writings, offering my apologies for presenting them in such condensed versions.

Hong Kong

On 20 November 1976 we landed at Hong Kong and were greeted by a group of Bahá'ís. Later, in one of the beautiful halls of the airport, a number of reporters interviewed me; the International Conference and the tenets of the Faith were discussed in great detail and photographs were also taken. We then went into the city. It was early evening and Hong Kong, immersed in the lights of its many streets and tall buildings, truly reminded one of the tales of the *Thousand and One Nights*.

Hong Kong had, at the end of 1966, a population of four million. Its inhabitants are ninety-nine per cent Chinese, the rest coming from Commonwealth countries with smaller groups of Americans, Portuguese, Filipinos, Dutch, Germans, French and Italians. Its official language is English, but many Chinese languages and dialects are spoken and Cantonese is universally understood. Its capital is Victoria.

Hong Kong is located off the Kwangtung coast of southern China, and consists of Hong Kong Island, Kowloon Peninsula, Stonecutters Island, and an area known as New Territories. It is one of the important centres of world commerce, and has marine and air connections with all the principal ports of the world. Such industries as fishing, shipbuilding, textiles and garments, and a number of light industries are well advanced.

It was my honour to represent the Universal House of Justice at the International Teaching Conference in Hong Kong, 27–30 November 1976, which was attended by more than five hundred Bahá'ís from such countries as Iran, India, Taiwan, Malaysia, Thailand, Indonesia, Philippine Islands, Japan, the United States, Canada, Italy, Denmark, Germany, Australia and others. Two other Hands of the Cause of God, Mr Featherstone and Dr Muhájir, and a number of members of the Auxiliary Boards were also present. (It was the fifth of eight International Teaching Conferences in 1976–7.)

The Message of the Universal House of Justice, especially that part which commented on the privileges and honours that Asia has received in the history of the Faith, deeply moved the believers and further prepared them for service to the Cause of God. This message may be read in *The Bahá'í World* (vol. XVII, pp. 135–6) but the following are a few of its significant words:

> What an imperishable glory has been bestowed upon the people of Asia, the first to be illumined by the rays of God's faith, the first recipients of His Call and the first promoters of His Cause . . . This great continent contains within its boundaries . . . not only the great majority of the human race but the great majority of the followers of Bahá'u'lláh. The potentiality of such a situation cannot be underestimated, nor must the great force latent within so large a proportion of the Army of Light be neglected . . .

The participation of the children in the Conference programme was one of the happiest ideas of the responsible committee. Also, the spirituality, sincerity and purity of heart of those beloved friends who, on the night commemorating the ascension of 'Abdu'l-Bahá, continued their prayers until after midnight, are truly unforgettable.

Upon the invitation of the National Spiritual Assembly of Hong Kong, a luncheon reception was held, and the Governor of Hong Kong and a number of scholars, newspaper editors and Bahá'ís attended. After the Governor had opened the programme, I spoke for half an hour on 'Education from a Bahá'í Perspective', my remarks being received with enthusiasm. After lunch, we three Hands of the Cause answered the questions of the journalists in a press conference.

Like other Bahá'í international events, and by the testimony of its participants, the Hong Kong Conference achieved high success.

The main points of my luncheon talk, with some of the extracts from Bahá'í writings which I used, are included in Appendix 1.

Japan

Japan (Nippon or Nihon) consists of four large islands and a great many smaller ones. One of its fascinating natural scenes is Mount Fujiyama (12,388 ft.) with its snow-covered summit, located near Kawaguchi Lake. A population of over one hundred and twenty million live in this country, of whom ninety-nine per cent are Japanese.

There is no single dominant religion, but the majority generally follow Buddhist rites, consider Confucius as a source of morality, and pay homage to Buddhist and Shinto deities alike.

The future of Japan was wonderfully portrayed by 'Abdu'l-Bahá in a Tablet to Mr Saichiro Fujita:

> Japan has made wonderful progress in material civilization, but she will become perfect when she will also make spiritual developments and the Power of the Kingdom become manifest in her.
>
> One will encounter a little difficulty in the beginning of the establishment of the Cause of God in that country, but later it will become very easy. For the inhabitants of Japan are intelligent, sagacious, and have the power of rapid assimilation. (*Japan Will Turn Ablaze*, p. 19. See also the quotation cited on p. 149.)

On 1 December, in the company of a number of Bahá'ís, we left Hong Kong for Japan and landed at Osaka airport.

The first two days were spent in meeting the friends, after which we participated in the National Teaching Conference of Japan, held in Kobe from 3 to 5 December. During the three days of the Conference two meetings were arranged, one for seekers and the other for parents, to whom I spoke in detail about education from a Bahá'í standpoint.

From Osaka we went to Kurashiki where a public meeting in a hotel drew an audience of sixty-one young seekers as well as a number of Bahá'ís. The following morning in a press conference I met six journalists to discuss the Faith. That same day we were received by the Mayor and I was also invited to address the Rotary Club, which he and some forty-eight prominent business men and civic leaders attended. By previous arrangement I again spoke about education in the Bahá'í Faith, a talk which was much praised and attracted the Mayor, the Superintendent of Education, and a few other well-known people to the Teachings.

In Hiroshima, now known as the 'City of Peace', a fireside meeting was held for seventy persons, thirty of whom were inquirers. The title of my lecture was 'Universal Peace in the Bahá'í Faith'.

My programme in Japan also included a fireside gathering in Kyoto with an attendance of fifty-nine (nineteen being non-Bahá'ís), a talk on 'The Harmony of Science and Religion' to a group of students in Osaka University, and two other meetings in Osaka and a neighbouring town. All these meetings were truly illumined and spirited, and were spent in the mention and praise of God.

In Tokyo I and Dr Muhájir consulted with the National Spiritual Assembly on ways of prosecuting the objectives of the Five Year Plan.

We finally returned to the Holy Land on 25 December 1976 via Hong Kong.

A description of two of the subjects I presented in the

various meetings is given in Appendix 1, entitled 'The Harmony of Science and Religion' and 'Suggestions for Teachers of Bahá'í Classes'.

In 1977, after ten days in Alaska, I flew on to Japan where I spent from 16 September to 10 October with a busy and fruitful schedule in which I spoke on twenty-four occasions in a dozen cities and towns and renewed my acquaintance with the Mayor of Kurashiki. One of the earlier visits was to Yamaguchi University School of Nursing, my subject before the student body being 'The Meaning of Life'. This was followed by a talk on 'The Meeting of Technology and Psychology' given before a large audience of both undergraduate and graduate students and professors at the university's School of Engineering. These are some lines from a report of this meeting: 'The atmosphere was a . . . serious and intellectual one . . . [He] established a firm intellectual framework of discussion for both subjects, and showed how true psychology bore the ultimate responsibility for the technical achievements of man – to enhance the livelihood of man and not to breed the means of his annihilation . . .'

There followed a three-day National Teaching Conference in Kurashiki in which I spoke nine times, some of my themes being on living a Bahá'í life, the education of children, Bahá'í marriage, and the elimination of prejudice, all pertinent to the conference theme of 'The Significance of Being a Bahá'í'. It is of interest that of the 95 persons attending, 49 were non-Bahá'ís.

The other places of my tour were Amagasaki, Ube, Takarazuka, Suita, Osaka, Kakogawa, Kyoto, Sendai and Tokyo. Local newspapers gave good publicity and many inquirers attended the meetings.

B. EUROPE

The summer months of 1975 were spent in service to the

Bahá'í summer schools of four countries. Leaving Haifa mid-June, I travelled to Norway, spent a few days in Oslo with the believers and in meeting young Bahá'í mothers to talk about the education of children, and then went on to the Summer School in Kristiansund, 1–9 July. Germany was my next stop, for the Summer School in a mountainous and delightful region named Sonnenberg/Harz, where I stayed until 20 July. Then came the Leicester Summer School in England attended by believers from eleven countries and invigorated by the presence of four Hands of the Cause of God, Mr Haney in the first week and Mr Faizí, Dr Muhájir and I in the second. In its cablegram to the School, the Universal House of Justice voiced its anticipation of an 'EFFECTIVE UPSURGE ACTIVITY RAPID ACHIEVEMENT GOALS PLAN' as a result of the courses; there were also sessions with the Hands of the Cause which were transferred to the lounges. Here is a passage from the report of this School which the friends left 'exhilarated and eager to serve the Cause':

> Mr Furútan stressed that our whole existence should be our responsibility – thinking, feeling, acting – all with prayer. He spoke of the recent developments at the World Centre of 'those world-shaking, world-embracing, world-directing administrative institutions'. With unforgettable stories he explained the station and infallibility of the House of Justice and the duties of the Hands who had been designated the 'chief stewards' by Shoghi Effendi.

Leaving England on 9 August I returned to the Continent to participate in the Swiss Summer School held in Ticino Canton close to Locarno, and remained with these dear friends until my departure at the end of the month for Turkey and thence to Haifa.

In these summer schools I taught a variety of courses centring on the Five Year Plan, the World Order of Bahá'u'lláh, historical subjects and the mysteries of the

Holy Books. Some of my material on the last of these I share with my readers in Appendix 1.

I returned to Germany and England two years later, June 1977, for conferences with Persian believers. In Mainz there were 513 present, and in London 1,600. The purpose and outcome of these conferences is best summed up in the cablegram sent to the Universal House of Justice from Mainz on 14 June:

> . . . WONDERFUL SPIRIT ENGENDERED JOYOUS LOVING ATMOSPHERE. CONSCIOUS VITAL NEEDS GOALS FIVE YEAR PLAN DETERMINED ARISE WIN VICTORIES GREATER SPEED. 18 BELIEVERS VOLUNTEERED TRAVEL TEACHING EUROPE 41 ABROAD INCLUDING AFRICA OUTPOURING RESOURCES EARMARKED TRAVEL TEACHING TEAMS COUNTRIES EUROPE . . .

Dr Muhájir was with me in Mainz as were two of the European Counsellors.

Before the close of the Five Year Plan and my visits to the European Bahá'ís during the period of these memoirs, I had the happy experience of being with both the Italian and Irish Bahá'ís in the summer of 1978, two of Europe's most lively and successful communities. The Summer School in Rimini, 2–10 September, had nearly 700 participants who gave splendid response to the need for pioneers and travelling teachers, filling all homefront goals during the school. My daily course on 'The Bahá'í Concept of Human Relations' dealt with the Bahá'í community, institutions of the Faith, the family and child education, and relations with non-Bahá'ís. The following is quoted from a report of my contribution:

> In psychology it is said that everything a man is, comes from his mind. If you want to change his behaviour, you must try to change his mind. One must try to understand why people behave in certain ways and have certain prejudices and ideas, then we can

begin to change these through the Teachings of Bahá'u'lláh. And how do we teach? 'Be a Bahá'í.'

At the Irish Summer School over 350 believers represented 14 countries. Their cablegram to the World Centre reported a heightening of the spirit of unity and consecration of their energies to the victory of the Five Year Plan, with first fruits in seven pioneer offers.

C. NORTH AMERICA

On the invitation of the National Spiritual Assembly of the Bahá'ís of the United States, and with the approval of the Universal House of Justice, I departed for the United States on 29 July 1976, arriving in Chicago after short stops in Rome, Athens and Paris. Before beginning our scheduled tour, I visited the Mashriqu'l-Adhkár, that masterpiece of architecture, and was greatly pleased, on the following morning, to meet the Hand of the Cause of God Mr Khádem and other friends in a gathering at the Temple.

Since a detailed account of my lectures and meetings during these forty-five days, and a description of the spirit of sacrifice and devotion demonstrated by the friends would unduly prolong this memoir, I mention below a brief outline of my activities.

Participated in the Summer School for Texas and Oklahoma, attended by 317 believers.

Met a total of 200 believers in Albuquerque, New Mexico, with three meetings for Bahá'í children, youth and adults.

Took part in the Summer School in the eastern part of the State of Washington, with 100 believers.

Met friends in San José, California and neighbouring areas, with more than 500 believers in one meeting.

Attended Bosch Summer School near Santa Cruz, California.

Visited the friends in Los Angeles, San Francisco and Carmel; there were over 1,000 Bahá'ís present in one of these meetings.

Attended Green Acre Summer School, in which 300 believers were present.

Met 380 believers in New York City.

Visited the Louis Gregory Institute for a few days and also the Bahá'ís of that area; the influence of that beloved Hand of the Cause was deeply felt by me. One meeting attracted over 80 Bahá'ís.

In Atlanta, Georgia and its suburbs, I met some 400 believers.

Returned to Wilmette for consultation with the National Spiritual Assembly and again visited the Mashriqu'l-Adhkár during meetings of prayer.

Participated in a meeting of some 80 believers in Chicago.

Met Spanish-speaking Bahá'ís of Wilmette.

Throughout this journey I was particularly pleased to note the growth of the Faith since my last visit in 1971 and commented several times, as reported, 'It is evident that you are teaching well, for everywhere I meet new believers. I would ask only that your teaching increase still more, for the time is ripe and many successes await your efforts.'

From 1977 until 1982 it was not possible for me to go again to the United States, Canada and Alaska, and so the paragraphs that follow describe my final services in 1977 to the Five Year Plan in that vast continent.

Our first engagement was attendance at the National Bahá'í Youth Conference in Champaign, Illinois, 29 June to 3 July, where we joined the Hands of the Cause of God Mr Khádem and Mr Sears. There were over 2,800 Bahá'í and non-Bahá'í youth there, and 'I felt and saw the deepest indications of joy and happiness in their faces, and praised

God for the magnitude of His Might and Power in that country' (from official report). During the conference we met 400 Persian believers resident in the United States.

After this, from 4 July until 3 September, we attended three summer schools in New York State, Asheville, North Carolina, and the Bosch Bahá'í School, spent three days at the Louis Gregory Bahá'í Institute, and met believers in some twenty localities, including New York, New Jersey, Denver, San Diego, Los Angeles and San Francisco, this last in its elegant and beautiful new Bahá'í Centre. While in Los Angeles I spoke at a meeting of over 1,000 believers and also met 500 Persian Bahá'ís from that area.

We then went on to Canada to attend a conference for the 'Commemoration of 'Abdu'l-Bahá's Visit to Montreal' for which about 500 believers gathered. After attending summer schools in Nova Scotia and Ontario, we travelled on to Saskatoon and Prince Albert, Saskatchewan, believers from nearby communities coming into Prince Albert for a one-day gathering. British Columbia was our next Province of call and here we visited the friends in Castlegar, Grand Forks and Nelson. A 45-minute television programme on child education was taped in Nelson for later broadcast. There was also a proclamation meeting for descendants of the Russian Dukhobors, whom I addressed in Russian.

And so to Alaska, for a National Teaching Conference in Anchorage, 10–11 September, with over 200 Bahá'ís present. Consultations were chiefly about the need for pioneers, travelling teaching teams, and consolidation in Alaskan villages. I was able to commend the believers in Alaska for their tireless teaching efforts which have gained them a well-deserved international reputation. My own talk was devoted to the education of children. Additionally, I travelled to meet believers in major Alaskan Bahá'í communities before departing for Japan on 16 September (see p. 183).

Bahá'í Summer School in Rimini, Italy, 2–10 September 1978

Alaskan Bahá'ís, Petersburg, 7–8 September 1977

In closing this chapter summarizing my travels during the Five Year Plan, I should like to quote lines which I wrote at the end of my American journey of 1977:

> . . . all throughout these meetings and summer schools, the highest degree of reverence, absolute certitude, and obedience . . . was manifested and evident. All the Counsellors, Auxiliary Board members and their assistants are sacrificially serving His Cause, the friends are becoming more and more familiar with these newly-born institutions, while the best possible relations exist between the Local Assemblies, the Counsellors, and the Auxiliary Board members.

From 1957 to this present time I have been residing in the Holy Land, and seize every opportunity to meet the pilgrims. Every year great numbers of friends from East and West attain the bounty of visiting the Holy Shrines and, as said by the beloved Guardian, the fresh blood of different Bahá'í communities continually rushes towards the heart of the Cause of God, and after its spiritual rejuvenation returns to its home.

A poignant reminder of their precious days at the World Centre has been lovingly conceived and prepared by Amatu'l-Bahá Rúḥíyyih Khánum in an original and beautiful film entitled *A Pilgrimage*, which has by now been shown in many Bahá'í communities around the world. Its appeal is not only to pilgrims, for its memorable views of all the scenes of pilgrimage which span the history of the Faith from the arrival of Bahá'u'lláh in the prison-city even to the construction of the Seat of The Universal House of Justice are sure to awaken in all hearts a desire to share in these sacred experiences.

In the course of these twenty-five years I have witnessed the arrival of thousands of people, Bahá'ís and others, at the Holy Shrines. One and all they have admired the beauty and exceptional designs of the gardens, and, in the words of the beloved Guardian, have had to confess their astonishment. This observation of every pilgrim that 'unless a believer visits the Holy Land himself to witness with his own eyes what the hand of the beloved Guardian has created, he can neither imagine the majesty and beauty of that paradise nor can he describe it to others', is in no way exaggerated. May the beloved friends be evermore privileged to attain this most great bounty.

Epilogue

The Universal House of Justice, in its message to the Bahá'ís of the World at Naw-Rúz 1979, described the achievements of the Five Year Plan in these words:

> The teaching victories in that Plan have been truly prodigious; the points of light, those localities where the Promised One is recognized, have increased from sixty-nine thousand five hundred to over ninety-six thousand; the number of Local Spiritual Assemblies has grown from seventeen thousand to over twenty-five thousand; eighteen new National Spiritual Assemblies have been formed . . .
>
> Beyond the expansion of the community, vital as it is, the Five Year Plan witnessed great progress in the spiritual development of the friends, the growing maturity and wisdom of Local and National Assemblies, and in the degree to which Bahá'í communities embody the distinguishing characteristics of Bahá'í life . . . This is the magnet which will attract the masses to the Cause of God, and the leaven that will transform human society.
>
> . . . We are the bearers of the Word of God in this day and, however dark the immediate horizons, we must go forward rejoicing in the knowledge that the work we are privileged to perform is God's work and will bring to birth a world whose splendour will outshine our brightest visions and surpass our highest hopes.

In the same message the announcement of a new Seven Year Plan, 1979–1986, was given. Although I could not leave the Holy Land after 1978, the opportunity of service at the World Centre was greatly increased, particularly in the development of the International Teaching Centre, and it has been my privilege to contribute in this field as well as being with the dear pilgrims.

However, towards the end of 1982 it became possible for me once again to return to the teaching field. From 18 September to 24 December I travelled in the United States and Canada, meeting both Eastern and Western friends in eighty-two meetings and speaking about the essential obligations of Bahá'ís. In addition to those gatherings I met the youth, children, mothers and other members of the families of martyrs in Iran, and these meetings with relatives of the martyrs were particularly very precious for me. I returned to Haifa on 30 December from whence I write these final lines.

During these last years the sad and unbearable news of the martyrdoms of so many dear friends in Iran who have given their lives with infinite love in the pathway of the Beloved, repeating and renewing the record of those dawn-breakers of the Heroic Age, has been announced in messages from the Universal House of Justice and recorded in letters and publications of the international Bahá'í community and in other books and journals. Like thousands of friends throughout the world, I have wept bitterly for such tragic events, and my prayers and supplications have been offered in the Holy Shrines for these courageous souls and for the patience and forbearance of their relatives and survivors. I am, however, convinced – as are Bahá'ís everywhere – that through the sacrifice of the pure blood of these martyr-heroes our beloved Faith will make tremendous progress in the world and fulfil completely all the divine promises.

Two weeks after my return to Haifa I was invited to recount to the friends at the World Centre some of the events of this American tour. The meeting was held in a hall of the Seat of the Universal House of Justice. It is fitting that my memoir should conclude in this way, for words cannot express the gratitude of my heart that I have lived to see the completion of this noble building, the permanent Seat occupied by the Universal House of Justice on 31 January

Four Hands of the Cause of God and other members of the International Teaching Centre, at the time of their first meeting, Bahá'í World Centre, 14 June 1973

The Hands of the Cause resident in Haifa, the members of the Universal House of Justice, and the Counsellor members of the International Teaching Centre on the steps of the Seat of the Universal House of Justice, 31 January 1983

1983. Their cable sent next day to 'followers of Bahá'u'lláh in every land' included these soul-stirring words:

LET ALL REJOICE. LET PRAISES ANCIENT BEAUTY RESOUND. MAY UNRELENTING EFFORTS FRIENDS EVERYWHERE HASTEN ADVENT THAT DAY WHEN WONDROUS POTENTIALITIES ENSHRINED IN TABLET CARMEL WILL BE FULLY REVEALED AND WHEN FROM GOD'S HOLY MOUNTAIN, AS ENVISAGED BELOVED GUARDIAN, WILL STREAM FORTH RIVERS OF LAWS AND ORDINANCES WITH ALL-CONQUERING POWER AND MAJESTY.

* * * * * * * *

I cannot close the pages of this book without adding a few words about my family, whose members throughout four generations have encouraged and supported me in my years of humble service to the Cause of Bahá'u'lláh. As I record their names my heart is filled with love and gratitude.

In Sabzivár my family consisted of my parents, my paternal grandmother, and four children: Muḥammad-Ḥusayn, 'Alí-Akbar, 'Alí-Aṣghar and 'Abbás-'Alí. In 'Ishqábád another child was added to our family who was named 'Atáu'lláh. (The names of my parents and grandmother are given in Chapter 1.)

My father and grandmother passed away in 'Ishqábád, and my mother in Tehran. Four of the children are living and are firm in the Covenant, by the grace of God.

In April 1931 I married a radiant and spiritual youth, Ataieh 'Azíz-i-Khurásání, the daughter of one of the old Bahá'í families of Iran. The fruits of this marriage are two daughters named Iran and Parvine.

Iran is the widow of Hand of the Cause of God Raḥmatu'lláh Muhájir, who died in Quito, Ecuador, in December 1979, and is a very active and confirmed believer in different fields of service. Both she and her beloved husband are Knights of Bahá'u'lláh. During my 1982 visit to North America, Iran accompanied and assisted me.

Parvine from the very beginning has been a lover of Bahá'í services, and has always exerted her utmost efforts in various fields.

Our family is also adorned with two granddaughters, Gisu and Shabnam. May they be, to their last breath, the handmaids of His sacred Threshold, and firm in His exalted Cause.

Appendix 1

Topics Discussed in Various Talks

A. INDIA, 1976

Faṣlu'l-Khiṭáb, or Decisive Decree

Faṣlu'l-Khiṭáb literally means a decree binding upon the two parties involved in a dispute.

In a religious context, the text of the Writings of the Manifestation of God and His laws as recorded in His Books are the Faṣlu'l-Khiṭáb. They are binding upon the believers and must be accepted by them with no doubts on their part as to the truth of these heavenly instructions.

The Blessed Beauty has said in the *Kitáb-i-Aqdas*: 'Well is it with him that hath turned thereunto, and apprehended the meaning of His decisive decree.' (Cited *Gleanings*, CLV.)

In the Bahá'í Dispensation the Bahá'ís have always had this heavenly bounty. At the time of the Báb, whatever was revealed by Him was the Faṣlu'l-Khiṭáb for the Bábís, and through His commands all differences were resolved. At the time of the Blessed Beauty, His commands, issuing from the heaven of His Will, were the Faṣlu'l-Khiṭáb for the believers and removed the source of all differences. At the time of the Centre of the Covenant, His utterances distinguished between truth and falsehood. And again, during the Guardianship of the beloved Shoghi Effendi, the primal branch, Faṣlu'l-Khiṭáb firmly governed the Bahá'í world community. Now the instructions of the Universal House of Justice, that supreme and infallible body, are the Faṣlu'l-Khiṭáb for the Bahá'ís of the world, as expressly revealed in the sacred Text. Its decisions, whatever they may be, are inspired by, and are from God. For this reason, in this blessed Dispensation the Religion of God is protected against division and sectarianism, and this Day shall not be followed by night. (See *God Passes By*, p. 99.)

Divinity can only be Approached through the Manifestations of God

The Báb has stated in the Persian *Bayán*:

Verily, whatsoever hath been revealed by God about attaining His presence or that of the Lord, is intended to be a reference to none other than Him Whom God shall make manifest inasmuch as God Himself cannot be seen. (III, 7.)

Whatsoever hath been mentioned in the Holy Books about attainment unto His Presence, referreth to the Presence of Him Who appeareth in His Manifestation; that is, He Who is the Point of Truth, Who is and hath been the Primal Will. (ibid.)

And those people whom thou seest calling upon God, and who, between themselves and God, think of themselves as virtuous, are, one and all, lost in the realms of their idle fancies and vain imaginings. They call upon One Who is unknown to them. (The Báb, *Kitáb-i-Panj-Sha'n*, p. 443.)

And the Blessed Beauty has said:

The essence of belief in Divine unity consisteth in regarding Him Who is the Manifestation of God and Him Who is the invisible, the inaccessible, the unknowable Essence as one and the same. By this is meant that whatever pertaineth to the former, all His acts and doings, whatever He ordaineth or forbiddeth, should be considered, in all their aspects, and under all circumstances, and without any reservation, as identical with the Will of God Himself. This is the loftiest station to which a true believer in the unity of God can ever hope to attain. Blessed is the man that reacheth this station, and is of them that are steadfast in their belief. (*Gleanings*, LXXXIV.)

. . . by 'attainment unto the divine Presence' is meant attainment unto the presence of His Beauty in the person of His Manifestation. (*Kitáb-i-Íqán*, p. 170.)

And if He, exalted be He, appeareth clothed in the raiment of man, this is by virtue of His mercy, so that His servants may not flee from Him, but may draw near unto Him, sit before the beauty of His Countenance, listen to His matchless melody, and be enchanted by what will stream forth from His tongue, and be revealed unto them from the heaven of His Will. (*Raḥíq-i-Ma<u>kh</u>túm*, vol. 2, p. 159.)

'Abdu'l-Bahá also states:

It is clear that if we wish to imagine the Reality of Divinity, this imagination is the surrounded, and we are the surrounding one; and it is sure that the one who surrounds is greater than the surrounded. From this it is certain and evident that if we imagine a Divine Reality outside of the Holy Manifestations, it is pure imagination, for there is no way to approach the Reality of Divinity which is not cut off to us, and all that we imagine is mere supposition.

Therefore, reflect that different peoples of the world are revolving around imaginations and are worshippers of the idols of thoughts and conjectures. They are not aware of this; they consider their imaginations to be the Reality which is withdrawn from all comprehension and purified from all descriptions. They regard themselves as the people of Unity, and the others as worshippers of idols; but idols at least have a mineral existence, while the idols of thoughts and the imaginations of man are fancies; they have not even mineral existence. 'Take heed ye who are endued with discernment.' (*Some Answered Questions*, p. 149.)

Miracles of the Manifestations of God

'Abdu'l-Bahá has also explained the significance of the miracles which are within the power of the Manifestations to perform:

The Holy Manifestations are the sources of miracles and the originators of wonderful signs . . . [but] for the Manifestations these miracles and wonderful signs have no importance; they do not even wish to mention them. For if we consider miracles a great proof, they are still only proofs and arguments for those who are present when they are performed, and not for those who are absent . . . The outward miracles have no importance for the people of Reality. If a blind man receive sight, for example, he will finally again become sightless, for he will die and be deprived of all his senses and powers . . . If the body of a dead person be resuscitated, of what use is it since the body will die again? . . . Wherever in the Holy Books they speak of raising the dead, the meaning is that the dead were blessed by eternal life; where it is said that the blind received sight, the signification is that he obtained the true perception; where it is said a deaf man received hearing, the meaning is that he acquired spiritual and heavenly hearing. This is ascertained from the text of the Gospel where Christ said: 'These are like those of whom Isaiah said, They have eyes and see not, they have ears and hear not; and I healed them.'

The meaning is not that the Manifestations are unable to perform miracles, for They have all power. But for Them inner sight, spiritual healing and eternal life are the valuable and important things. (ibid. pp. 100–102.)

In the same way, His resurrection from the interior of the earth is also symbolical; it is a spiritual and divine fact, and not material; and likewise His ascension to heaven is a spiritual and not material ascension.

Beside these explanations, it has been established and proved by science that the visible heaven is a limitless area, void and empty, where innumerable stars and planets revolve . . . this subject of the ascension of Christ with an elemental body to the visible heaven is contrary to the science of mathematics . . . (ibid. pp. 104–5.)

Also, most of the miracles of the Prophets which are mentioned have an inner significance. For instance, in the Gospel it is written that at the martyrdom of Christ darkness prevailed, and the earth quaked, and the veil of the Temple was rent in twain from the top to the bottom, and the dead came forth from their graves. If these events had happened, they would indeed have been awesome, and would certainly have been recorded in the history of the times. They would have become the cause of much troublings of heart. Either the soldiers would have taken down Christ from the cross, or they would have fled. These events are not related in any history; therefore, it is evident they ought not to be taken literally, but as having an inner significance.

Our purpose is not to deny such miracles; our only meaning is that they do not constitute decisive proofs, and that they have an inner significance. (ibid. pp. 37–8.)

The Administrative Order of the Faith of Bahá'u'lláh

The beloved Guardian, in *The Dispensation of Bahá'u'lláh* (see *The World Order of Bahá'u'lláh*, pp. 97–119), has clearly described the essential elements of the Administrative Order, its origins, its distinction from religious institutions of the past, its twin pillars and their relationship, the theory on which it is based in contrast to the three recognized forms of secular government (democracy, autocracy and aristocracy), its vitality and unique character, and its consummation with 'the advent of that golden millennium – the Day when the kingdoms of this world shall have become the Kingdom of God Himself, the Kingdom of Bahá'u'lláh'.

Since the Guardian's purpose in writing this tremendous document was to 'lay special stress . . . upon certain truths which lie at the basis of our Faith and the integrity of which it is our first duty to safeguard' (ibid. p. 99), I devoted one of my talks in India to the Administrative Order. Because the Guardian's own words are available to my English readers, as they were not to my Persian readers when I first composed these memoirs, I do not now summarize my remarks, but urge all Bahá'ís to study the pages mentioned above.

The Benefit of Happiness

The Báb, in the Persian *Bayán*, states:

In the Bayán no act of worship is nearer unto His acceptance than bringing joy to the hearts of the believers, and none more remote than inflicting sorrow upon them. (VII, 18.)

The importance of happiness and joy to our spiritual and physical well-being was frequently expressed by 'Abdu'l-Bahá. Here are eight extracts from His writings and talks which illustrate this theme. (The translations of all have been approved by the Bahá'í World Centre and the last four extracts may be found in Maḥmúd's Diary.)

At the Threshold of the one true God no act is more meritorious than imparting happiness to the hearts of the friends. Each one of the friends should, most willingly, endeavour to bring happiness, joy and gladness to those with whom he associates.

Be not perturbed, grieved or angry because all these are harmful. Rather, live ye your days happily and joyously so that 'Abdu'l-Bahá may rejoice in the happiness of the friends, and his weakness may be reduced.

For 'Abdu'l-Bahá, the health of the friends comes before and is more important than his own.

The best food is happiness.

Happiness influenceth the preservation of health, but sorrow causeth various diseases. (vol. 1, p. 129.)

Act ye in such wise as to impart happiness to me, then ye shall witness the results. (vol. 1, p. 270.)

Be ye always the source of happiness to the hearts, for, the best of men is one who winneth the hearts and refraineth from troubling any soul, and the worst of men is one who vexeth the hearts and causeth people to be grieved. Always endeavour to gladden the people and to rejoice their hearts so that ye may be enabled to guide them. (vol. 1, p. 272.)

Be ye always the bearers of good tidings and spread such news quickly . . . On the other hand, if ye have a bad message or news for a certain person, show ye no haste in conveying it, and trouble not the heart of the concerned individual. When I have bad news for someone, I do not convey it to him openly, rather do I converse with him in such wise that when he heareth that news, my words bring comfort to him. (vol. 2, p. 308.)

B. HONG KONG, 1976

Education from a Bahá'í Perspective

The following extracts from the words of 'Abdu'l-Bahá are a brief summary of the Bahá'í attitude towards education:

When we consider existence, we see that the mineral, vegetable, animal and human worlds are all in need of an educator . . . If there were no educator, there would be no such things as comforts, civilization or humanity. If a man be left alone in a wilderness where he sees none of his own kind, he will undoubtedly become a mere brute; it is then clear that an educator is needed.

But education is of three kinds: material, human and spiritual. Material education is concerned with the progress and development of the body, through gaining its sustenance, its material comfort and ease . . .

Human education signifies civilization and progress . . .

Divine education is that of the Kingdom of God: it consists in acquiring divine perfections, and this is true education . . . (*Some Answered Questions*, pp. 7–8.)

If the character is not trained, the sciences shall cause harm. Science and knowledge are laudable, if they are complemented by a praiseworthy character and behaviour. Otherwise they shall be a deadly poison, a dreadful disaster. A vicious and deceitful physician can cause havoc and the onset of a variety of diseases . . . The foundation of schools should be based primarily on training in good manners and morals, and on the development of praiseworthy conduct and behaviour. (*Payám-i-Malakút*, pp. 215–16.)

Bahá'u'lláh hath proclaimed the universality of education, which is essential to the unity of mankind, that one and all may be equally educated, whether girls or boys, and receive the same education. When education is universalized in all schools, perfect communication between the members of the human race will be established. When all receive the same kind of education the foundations of war and contention will be utterly destroyed. (*Khaṭábát-i-Mubárakih*, p. 232.)

Educators and psychologists, American, European and Asian, generally agree that education plays a major role in the formation of human behaviour. John Locke states that the inner nature of a child is so pure that a teacher, by education, can impress on it whatever he likes, irrespective of inherited characteristics. It has been said that 'Knowledge received in childhood is like an engraving made on stone'.

Of course, heredity and innate characteristics are important factors, but education is the foundation of morals and praiseworthy attributes. Whatever parents in their homes teach their children or instructors in schools and universities convey to their students, and whatever the influences of the environment – such as talk they hear at home and in educational institutions, the newspapers they read, or the programmes they watch on television – the morals, beliefs and characters of children and youth are being formed thereby.

In the words of Shoghi Effendi:

> We must therefore rise to serve the members of the human race and educate first the individuals, so that the nations, which are composed of individuals, and the governments, which belong to these nations, may both be converted and guided, and that through this agency the unity of mankind may be established and its prosperity and success realized. (Cited by Ishráq-i-Khávarí, *Má'idiy-i-Ásmání*, vol. 3, p. 47.)

Therefore, if we want men to scorn war and bloodshed, and establish peace and eliminate their useless prejudices, we should educate our children from a very early age, in all the schools of the world, in the basic unity of mankind. They should be protected against such doctrines as the inevitability of the 'struggle for existence' which is particular to the animal kingdom, and an exaggerated nationalism whereby the people of other countries are considered as strangers only; instead, the love of country and mankind as a whole, without racial, national and similar prejudices, should be implanted in their hearts.

An effect cannot exist without a cause. When we review the history of mankind and analyse impartially the unwholesome events and devastating wars that have always stained the earth with the blood of its inhabitants, we realize that the fundamental cause of all these events has been religious, national or racial prejudice. These prejudices, which are constantly reinforced in people from childhood to the end of their lives, have always succeeded in engaging men in one dispute or another.

For example, it is recorded that the Babylonians massacred 50,000 of their women in dread of their captivity. Another tribe killed their parents with their own hands in fear of Alexander the Great. The people of Sidon, in 541 BC, witnessed the self-inflicted burning of 400,000 inhabitants of that city. The savagery of Genghiz Khan and Timur (Tamerlane), during whose reigns millions of innocent people were massacred, is well known to everyone and does not require a lengthy description.

Moreover, during the First World War ten million people were killed, in addition to another fifteen million who suffered various injuries. Similarly, in the Second World War thirty-two million were killed, thirty million injured, and twelve million were held in prison camps. To visualize the severity of the event, your attention is drawn to the following statistics incurred by just one of the countries involved in this war:

17	million people were killed
20	million lost their homes
20	million children were orphaned
200	million animals were either killed or injured
100	million books were burned
84,000	schools were destroyed
70	cities were ruined
3,000	factories were destroyed

Such are the results of war. Will Durant, author of *The Story of Civilization*, writes that during the past 4,000 years only 268 years have passed without wars. Another scholar estimates that in the period of 6,000 years of recorded history, only 292 years have been spent in peace.

To return to our topic, if we wish to remove an effect, its cause has to be eliminated. To establish peace in the world, the methods of education must be changed so that future generations are imbued with a spirit of unity and concord and warned against estrangement. This utterance of Bahá'u'lláh should be the foundation of education: 'O well beloved ones! The tabernacle of unity hath been raised; regard ye not one another as strangers. Ye are the fruits of one tree, and the leaves of one branch.' (*Tablets of Bahá'u'lláh*, p. 164.)

C. JAPAN, 1976

The Harmony of Science and Religion (University of Osaka)

Scholars have recognized two categories of knowledge acquired by human beings: common and scientific. The former results from daily experience without any attempt to relate one event to another. The scope of 'common knowledge' is neither unified nor all-embracing. It does not lead to firm conclusions because its information is isolated and haphazard, likely to change as the sequence of events changes.

Scientific knowledge, on the other hand, is acquired by purposive investigation of the problem under research, the collection of data based on controlled experiment and logical and mathematical principles, the discovery of the nature and relationships of the various components, and the establishment of a sequence of events according to cause and effect.

Every branch of scientific research follows four stages: (a) the collection of relevant data, (b) systematic organization of this data and the development and testing of hypotheses, (c) discovery and formulation of specific laws, and (d) the framing of general laws based on the accumulation of specific laws and their relationships. The more a science is based on universal or general laws, the more exact and reliable it will be.

In the Bahá'í Faith religion is defined as follows:*

Religion . . . is the necessary connection which emanates from the reality of things; and as the supreme Manifestations of God are aware of the mysteries of beings, therefore, They understand this essential connection, and by this knowledge establish the Law of God. (*Some Answered Questions*, p. 159.)

On the other hand, science is defined thus:

The greatest attainment in the world of humanity has ever been scientific in nature. It is the discovery of the realities of things. (*The Promulgation of Universal Peace*, p. 348.)

Concerning the harmony of science and religion these words have been revealed:

Religion and science are linked together; they cannot be separated. (*Khaṭábát-i-'Abdu'l-Bahá*, p. 32.)

Religion and reason are the same; they cannot be separated from each other. (ibid. p. 227.)

Religion and science walk hand in hand, and any religion contrary to science is not the truth. (*Paris Talks*, p. 131.)

Science and reason are light; religion must be in harmony with science and reason. (*Khaṭábát-i-'Abdu'l-Bahá*, p. 225.)

. . . science is the light, and, being so, religion *truly* so called does not oppose knowledge. (*Paris Talks*, p. 144.)

The greatest bounty of God to man is knowledge . . . If religious beliefs should contradict science and reason, they are assuredly ignorance. (*Khaṭábát-i-'Abdu'l-Bahá*, p. 226.)

Any religion that contradicts science or that is opposed to it, is only ignorance – for ignorance is the opposite of knowledge . . . Whatever the intelligence of man cannot understand, religion ought not to accept. Religion and science walk hand in hand, and any religion contrary to science is not the truth. (*Paris Talks*, pp. 130–31.)

* The texts quoted in this topic are from the writings and talks of 'Abdu'l-Bahá.

. . . for God, knowledge is the most glorious gift of man and the most noble of human perfections. (*Some Answered Questions*, p. 137.)

Science is the discoverer of truth, and the religions of God contain the whole truth. (*Khaṭábát-i-Mubárakih*, p. 64.)

Suggestions for Teachers of Bahá'í Classes

One of the most difficult tasks in the education of children is answering their questions in an appropriate way. Many books have been written on the subject and many methods have been discussed, but as yet no conclusive answer has been found. For if the teacher decides to answer all their questions accurately, their level of understanding and education will prevent them at times from comprehending some of the answers. How is it possible for a child to grasp the answers to questions that learned philosophers are unable to resolve? In the words of 'Abdu'l-Bahá:

A small child cannot comprehend the laws that govern nature, but this is on account of the immature intellect of that child; when he is grown older and has been educated he too will understand the everlasting truths. (*Paris Talks*, p. 145.)

But if the teacher decides to respond inaccurately to the child by citing childish or fictional answers, he will adversely affect his thoughts and spirit.

Therefore, this task is not an easy one. Discussion with children on these matters (i.e. universal principles) must be done by expert educators, and that only with utmost caution. It requires an introduction to the subject and a conclusion. For example, before entering a full discussion, children should be reminded that there are numerous things existing in the world which we cannot see. To clarify the matter, one can use a small radio and say: 'While we are in this room, from radio stations all around the world waves of music, news, talks, etc. are sent here to this very room, but we can neither see nor hear them. However, if we turn this radio on, we can hear different programmes on different wave lengths. Therefore, we cannot say that because we don't see or hear something, it doesn't exist. We cannot see many things from far away, but with binoculars and telescope we can bring them closer and see them. Also, sometimes we see things as very small, although in reality they are very large. For instance, when we look at the stars at night we see them as small as a walnut shell and even smaller, while they are a thousand times larger than our planet.'

With such examples the minds of the children should be prepared. One of the most important matters in the education of children is that they should understand and feel that they cannot comprehend everything in childhood, and that they should have patience, go to kindergarten, school, high school and university to mature in their intelligence. They can be told that a child, in his early years, is physically unable to lift heavy objects. However, when the same child grows, exercises and gains strength, he will be able to lift even very heavy weights. This point can be easily demonstrated by asking the child to lift a heavy weight, then assuring him that by giving himself time to grow he will be able to lift it.

It is the same with the understanding of different subjects which the child is unable to comprehend in childhood. If children ask questions beyond their level of comprehension, the teachers should reply kindly, offering them a few examples such as those cited above, and assuring them that as they will have to learn gradually different lessons in school, in the same way they will understand gradually the difficult subjects.

I would like to stress again that this is a very delicate matter which cannot be explained easily, especially in weekly Bahá'í classes when children are present only one hour per week, and often the teachers of these classes are not professional educators.

Usually, the lesser danger is to approach difficult questions with caution, postponing answers for the future when the children will have developed the facility to comprehend complex matters.

D. EUROPE, 1975

The Difficulty of Translation

'Abdu'l-Bahá has said: 'Truly translation is very difficult. One has to have the utmost proficiency in science and religion, in divine wisdom, in the current trends of thought in Europe, and in philosophical and scientific terms.' (*Má'idiy-i-Ásmání*, vol. 9, p. 141.) When the translator lacks such knowledge and understanding, mistakes are bound to occur.

For example, 'Abdu'l-Bahá has interpreted the verse of the Qur'án: 'I swear by the Fig and by the olive, by Mount Sinai, and by this inviolate soil!' (XCV:1–3.) As demonstrated in this translation by Rodwell, all the translators of this passage have literally translated 'Tín' and 'Zaytún' as 'fig' and 'olive', respectively. But here is the interpretation of the Master:

> Tíná and Zaitá are outwardly two hills in Jerusalem on which divine revelation was sent to the prophets of God . . . By the mount of Tíná the reality of Christ is intended, and by the mount of Zaitá, the reality of Muḥammad . . . Tíná and Zaitá in the Hebrew language are Tín and Zaytún [i.e. in Arabic]. (Translation approved by the Bahá'í World Centre.)

The Four Gospels

Bahá'u'lláh has said: 'The four Gospels were written after Him [Christ]. John, Luke, Mark and Matthew – these four wrote after Christ what they remembered of His utterances.' (Ishráq-i-Khávarí, *Muḥáḍarát*, vol. 1, p. 366.)

And 'Abdu'l-Bahá has given further explanation:

> . . . as it is known, the Gospels were written only in Hebrew and Greek, and not even in the language of the Romans [Latin], although it was at the time the official language. As the disciples were not well-versed in it, the Gospels were not written in that language. (Ishráq-i-Khávarí, *Má'idiy-i-Ásmání*, vol. 9, p. 22.)

Matthew was one of the disciples, and evidently wrote his Gospel some time after Mark's for Jewish people in the Levant.

The real name of Mark was John, son of Mary; the disciples used to gather in his house in Jerusalem. He was the companion and translator of Peter and Barnabas, from whom he probably obtained some of the content of his Gospel, writing it in Rome for Roman Christians. It is believed to have been written about AD 65.

Luke was a Greek physician and was the travelling companion of Paul. He wrote his Gospel in Greek with Paul's guidance, about AD 85. It is generally accepted that he was also the author of 'The Acts of the Apostles'.

John, the brother of James, wrote his Gospel in Ephesus in old age, probably about AD 100, and passed away in his nineties.

As readers will know, there has been much scholarly research into the dating of the Four Gospels and opinions are by no means united.

There are also several ancient and valuable manuscripts which have assisted translators of the Gospels to get nearer to the actual words of their authors. The oldest of these is the Codex Sinaiticus, a fourth-century document which has been kept in the British Museum. Two others are the Codex Vaticanus, held in the Vatican, and Codex Alexandrinus. (A Codex is a manuscript in book form, unlike the scroll used in the time of Christ.)

The term 'Evangel' is derived from the Greek meaning 'bringing good news'; it is used in the sense of a message of glad tidings. It was a synonym in earlier centuries for 'gospel', but its use in this way is now considered rhetorical or archaic. Alternate meanings have included the record of Christ's life as contained in the Four Gospels, religious teaching contained in the New Testament, or one of the Four Gospels itself.

In the Qur'án the term is mentioned at least eleven times: 'Ingil' means 'Evangel'. Here are these references according to Rodwell:

'The Family of Imran'—III:2,43,58
'The Table'—V:50,51,70,72,110
'Al Araf'—VII:156
'The Victory'—XLVIII:29
'Iron'—LVII:27

Sons of God

Bahá'u'lláh states: 'In former Holy Books, God hath called His servants, one and all, His sons.' (*Iqtidárát*, p. 4.)

And 'Abdu'l-Bahá tells us:

> The designation of 'son of God' at the time of Moses and Christ was a term which was used also in relation to the Children of Israel, as in the Torah they have been called 'sons of God'. In Exodus at the end of chapter four, God said unto Moses to inform Pharaoh that 'the children of Israel are my first-born sons. If thou wilt not free them, I will slay thy first-born son.' (Maḥmúd's Diary, vol. 2, p. 361.)

The following references are mentioned for further clarification:

Psalms 2:7
Genesis 6:2

The Book of Job 1:6; 2:1, 38:7
Exodus 4:22–3
Matthew 5:9
John 1:12–13

Prohibition of Alcohol

There is a tradition in Islam from Imam Riḍá which states: 'God doth not send a Prophet except with prohibition of alcohol.'

In all the religions of the past, alcohol has either been forbidden directly and categorically, or has been emphatically scorned and blamed. The following few references from the Holy Books are noteworthy:

Old Testament	Leviticus 10:9
	Deuteronomy 21:20–21
	Proverbs 20:1, 23:20, 29–32
	Joel 1:5
	Habakkuk 2:5, 15–16
	Numbers 6:1–4
	Isaiah 5:11–12,22–3; 28:1–3,7
	Judges 13:4,14
New Testament	Galatians 5:21
	Ephesians 5:18
	I Corinthians 5:11; 6:10
	Romans 14:21
	Luke 21:34
Qur'án	II:216; IV:46; V:92

In the Bahá'í Faith the prohibition of alcohol is so definite that it is not necessary to give many references, but the reader may refer to *The Advent of Divine Justice* by Shoghi Effendi, p. 27, for statements by Bahá'u'lláh and 'Abdu'l-Bahá. Persian friends may also consult the *Lawḥ-i-Rám* by Bahá'u'lláh.

The Spiritual Meaning of Some of the Terms used in the Bible

'Abdu'l-Bahá has explained in *Some Answered Questions*, chapter 16, why intellectual and spiritual conceptions must be expressed in outward forms and symbols. His words are indeed the key needed by all who wish to understand the spiritual meanings contained in the Holy Books. The following references are to such symbolic terms, as well as to several other points of interest:

Dead – Matthew 8:21–2
Heaven – John 3:13,31; 6:38
Resurrection and Life – John 11:25,37–44
Manna – John 6:30–36,48–58
Blind and Seeing – John 9:39–41
Bread and Wine – Matthew 26:26–8
Meeting of Christ with Moses and Elias – Luke 9:30–36
Existence of Christ before Abraham – John 8:51–8
Peace – Matthew 10:34; Luke 12:51; 22:36–8
Mother and Brother – Matthew 12:46–50; Mark 3:31–5; Luke 8:19–21
The Siblings of Christ – Matthew 13:55

False Prophets

In Matthew 7:15 it is said: 'Beware of false prophets, which come to you in sheep's clothing, but inwardly they are ravening wolves.'

In the Bible, five ranks have been fixed to guide the believers: apostles, prophets, evangelists, pastors and teachers. This is stated in the Epistle of Paul to the Ephesians:

> He that descended is the same also that ascended up far above all heavens, that he might fill all things. And he gave some, apostles; and some, prophets; and some, evangelists; and some, pastors

and teachers. For the perfecting of the saints, for the work of the ministry, for the edifying of the body of Christ . . . (4:10–12.)

Also in the First Epistle of Paul to the Corinthians it is mentioned:

And God hath set some in the church, first apostles, secondarily prophets, thirdly teachers, after that miracles, then gifts of healings, helps, governments, diversities of tongues. (12:28)

We realize, therefore, that the prophets, in the language of the Bible, are one of the categories of servants of the church, their rank being after the apostles, and this term (prophet) has never been attributed to the independent Manifestation of God.

In Matthew 23:34 it is also mentioned:

Wherefore, behold, I send unto you prophets, and wise men, and scribes: and some of them ye shall kill and crucify; and some of them shall ye scourge in your synagogues, and persecute them from city to city.

Therefore, it is evident that His Holiness Christ has considered the prophets in the same rank with the 'wise' and the 'scribes'. Further study of the following references will assist in understanding this matter:

II Peter 2:16
Acts 13:1; 15:32; 21:10–13
I Corinthians 11:4–5
Titus 1:12

The Qur'án

The Qur'án has also been called Furqán, Tanzíl, Dhikr, Ḥikmat, and Kitáb. Each of these is a common name also used in other contexts. The adjectives attributed to the

Qur'án, taken from the Book of God itself, are as follows: Karím (generous), 'Azím (majestic), Majíd (glorious), Mubín (perspicuous) and Ghayr-i-Dhí-'Awaj (free of error).

According to the researches of Muslim scholars, the Qur'án has 114 chapters (suras), 6,236 verses, 76,442 words and 326,671 letters. Most Muslim historians are of the opinion that the verses of the Qur'án, following their revelation, were transcribed on the instructions of the Prophet Himself. There were forty-one amanuenses who would transcribe the verses and offer them to the Prophet. Then the believers would memorize the verses, or write them down on skins or the leaves of palm trees, or engrave them on stones and bones.

During the lifetime of Muḥammad, the verses of the Qur'án were collected by five persons: 'Alí ibn Abí-Ṭálib, Mu'ádh ibn Jabalih, Abí ibn Ka'b, Zayd ibn Thábit and Abú Zayd. After the ascension of Muḥammad, His son-in-law 'Alí remained at home for a few days to collect the Qur'án. When 'Uthmán became caliph, he appointed a number of experts who arranged the order of the Qur'án in the version now universally used. Scholars also believe that 318 non-Arabic terms have been revealed in the Qur'án. (See Jeffery, *The Foreign Vocabulary of the Qur'án*.)

Study of *Lawḥ-i-Qiná*, addressed by Bahá'u'lláh to Ḥájí Muḥammad-Karím Khán-i-Kirmání, and of *Fará'id* by Mírzá Abu'l-Faḍl (particularly pp. 538–40 and 468–77) will supplement this information.

Each of the chapters of the Qur'án is given a title having direct relationship to the verses revealed in that chapter; for example, 'The Family of Imran', 'The Women', etc.

The Old Testament

The Torah (literally, Law), originally in Hebrew, consists of the Five Books of Moses, also known as the Pentateuch. In the Book of Joshua it is said:

> Be ye therefore very courageous to keep and to do all that is written in the book of the law of Moses, that ye turn not aside therefrom to the right hand or to the left. (23:6.)

And in Deuteronomy:

> When all Israel is come to appear before the Lord thy God in the place which he shall choose, thou shalt read this law before all Israel in their hearing. Gather the people together, men and women, and children, and the stranger that is within thy gates, that they may hear, and that they may learn, and fear the Lord your God, and observe to do all the words of this law. (31:11–12.)
>
> . . . Moses commanded the Levites, which bare the ark of the covenant of the Lord, saying, Take this book of the law, and put it in the side of the ark of the covenant of the Lord your God, that it may be there for a witness against thee. (31:25–6.)

The ascension of Moses has been given in detail in Deuteronomy 32:48–52 and 34:5–9.

The Old Testament is divided into four categories: the Five Books of the Torah, historical accounts, exhortations and admonitions, and the Books of the Prophets of Israel. It was translated into Aramaic, Greek, Syriac, Ethiopic, Armenian, Coptic and Latin during the centuries between the 3rd BC and the 7th AD. The most important Arabic version was made about AD 900. There have been innumerable translations since the fourteenth century.

The first complete English translation of the Old and New Testaments was made in 1382, and since the beginning of the 19th century, through the extension of Christian missionary activity, translations of the complete Bible or portions of it into the languages of the world have multiplied; by 1950 these had reached a thousand and work is still continuing.

Appendix 2

Countries Visited in My Travels

Africa
Egypt
Ethiopia (incl. Eritrea)
Kenya
Sudan
Tanzania
Uganda

Asia
Ceylon (Sri Lanka)
Cyprus
Hong Kong
India
Indonesia
Iran
Japan
Korea, South
Malaysia (Singapore)
Nepal
Pakistan
Philippines
Turkey

Australasia
Australia (incl. Tasmania)
New Zealand

Europe
Austria
Belgium
Denmark
Finland
France (incl. Monaco)
Germany, West
Greece
Irish Republic
Italy (incl. San Marino)
Luxemburg
Netherlands
Norway
Portugal
Spain
Sweden
Switzerland
United Kingdom (incl. Wales)

North America
Canada
United States (incl. Alaska, Hawaii)

South America
Argentina
Brazil
Uruguay

Bibliography

‘ABDU’L-BAHÁ. *Khaṭábát-i-‘Abdu’l-Bahá*. Cairo: Faraju’lláh Dhakí Kurdí, vol. 1, 1921.

—— *Khaṭábát-i-Mubárakih*. Tehran: (no details), BE 99.

—— *Memorials of the Faithful*. Translated and annotated by Marzieh Gail. Wilmette, Illinois: Bahá’í Publishing Trust, 1971.

—— *Paris Talks*. London: Bahá’í Publishing Trust, 12th edn 1971.

—— *The Promulgation of Universal Peace*. Compiled by Howard MacNutt. Wilmette, Illinois: Bahá’í Publishing Trust, 2nd edn 1982.

—— *The Secret of Divine Civilization*. Translated by Marzieh Gail in consultation with Ali-Kuli Khan. Wilmette, Illinois: Bahá’í Publishing Trust, 2nd edn 1970.

—— *Selections from the Writings of ‘Abdu’l-Bahá*. Translated by a Committee at the Bahá’í World Centre and by Marzieh Gail. Haifa: Bahá’í World Centre, 1978.

—— *Some Answered Questions*. Collected and translated from the Persian by Laura Clifford Barney. Wilmette, Illinois: Bahá’í Publishing Trust, 4th rev. edn 1981.

—— *Tablets of the Divine Plan, revealed by ‘Abdu’l-Bahá to the North American Bahá’ís*. Wilmette, Illinois: Bahá’í Publishing Trust, rev. edn. 1977.

ABU’L-FAḌL, MÍRZÁ. *Kitábu’l-Fará’id*. Cairo, undated. Written in AH 1315 (AD 1899).

Alaska Bahá’í News. Published by the National Spiritual Assembly of the Bahá’ís of Alaska.

Bahá’í Education: A Compilation. Compiled by the Research Department of the Universal House of Justice. Wilmette, Illinois: Bahá’í Publishing Trust, 1977. (Also published by Bahá’í Publishing Trust, Oakham, England.)

Bahá’í Holy Places. Haifa: Bahá’í World Centre, 1968.

Bahá’í International News Service. News of the Bahá’í World Community issued by the Bahá’í World Centre.

Bahá’í News. Published monthly by the National Spiritual Assembly of the Bahá’ís of the United States, Wilmette, Illinois.

Bahá'í World, The. An International Record.

Vol. VI. 1934–1936. Wilmette, Illinois: Bahá'í Publishing Trust, repr. 1980.

Vol. IX. 1940–1944. Wilmette, Illinois: Bahá'í Publishing Trust, repr. 1981.

Vol. XII. 1950–1954. Wilmette, Illinois: Bahá'í Publishing Trust, repr. 1981.

Vol. XIII. 1954–1963. Haifa: Bahá'í World Centre, 1970.

Vol. XIV. 1963–1968. Haifa: Bahá'í World Centre, 1974.

Vol. XV. 1968–1973. Haifa: Bahá'í World Centre, 1976.

Vol. XVII. 1976–1979. Haifa: Bahá'í World Centre, 1981.

BAHÁ'U'LLÁH. *Epistle to the Son of the Wolf*. Translated by Shoghi Effendi. Wilmette, Illinois: Bahá'í Publishing Trust, rev. edn. 1976.

—— *Gleanings from the Writings of Bahá'u'lláh*. Translated by Shoghi Effendi. Wilmette, Illinois: Bahá'í Publishing Trust, rev. edn 1978.

—— *Iqtidárát*. A compilation of the Tablets of Bahá'u'lláh. AH 1310.

—— *Kitáb-i-Aqdas*. See *Synopsis and Codification of the Laws and Ordinances of the Kitáb-i-Aqdas*.

—— *Kitáb-i-Íqán. The Book of Certitude*. Translated by Shoghi Effendi. Wilmette, Illinois: Bahá'í Publishing Trust, rev. edn 1974.

—— *Lawḥ-i-Sulṭán*. Tablet to the Sháh of Persia. See *The Proclamation of Bahá'u'lláh* and Shoghi Effendi, *The Promised Day Is Come*. A translation in full by E. G. Browne is included in *A Traveller's Narrative*, pp. 108–51 and Note X. (See below for these titles.)

—— *The Proclamation of Bahá'u'lláh to the Kings and Leaders of the World*. Haifa: Bahá'í World Centre, 1967.

—— *Súriy-i-Mulúk*. See *The Proclamation of Bahá'u'lláh* and Shoghi Effendi, *The Promised Day is Come*, for extracts translated by Shoghi Effendi.

—— *Tablets of Bahá'u'lláh revealed after the Kitáb-i-Aqdas*. Translated by Habib Taherzadeh with the assistance of a Committee at the Bahá'í World Centre. Haifa: Bahá'í World Centre, 1978.

BALYUZI, H. M. *'Abdu'l-Bahá. The Centre of the Covenant of Bahá'u'lláh*. Oxford: George Ronald, 1971.

—— *The Báb. The Herald of the Day of Days*. Oxford: George Ronald, 1973.

—— *Edward Granville Browne and the Bahá'í Faith*. Oxford: George Ronald, repr. 1980.

BROWNE, E. G. (ed.). *A Traveller's Narrative written to illustrate the Episode of the Báb*. English Translation and Notes. Cambridge University Press, vol. 2, 1891.

ESSLEMONT, J. E. *Bahá'u'lláh and the New Era*. Wilmette, Illinois: Bahá'í Publishing Trust, 4th rev. edn 1975.

Furútan, A.-A. *Ḥikáyat-i-Dil* (The Story of My Heart). Oxford: George Ronald, 1981.

—— *Mothers, Fathers and Children.* Oxford: George Ronald, repr. 1982.

Giachery, Ugo. *Shoghi Effendi – Recollections.* Oxford: George Ronald, 1973.

Ḥaydar-'Alí, Ḥájí Mírzá. *Bihjatu'ṣ-Ṣudúr.* Bombay: 1913.

Is͟hráq-i-K͟hávarí, 'Abdu'l-Ḥamíd. *Má'idiy-i-Ásmání.* Tehran: Bahá'í Publishing Trust, vols. 3 and 9, BE 129.

—— *Muḥáḍirát.* Tehran: Bahá'í Publishing Trust, vol. 1, BE 120.

—— *Payám-i-Malakút.* Tehran: Bahá'í Publishing Trust, BE 130.

—— *Raḥíq-i-Mak͟htúm.* Tehran: Bahá'í Publishing Trust, vol. 2, BE 131.

Japan Will Turn Ablaze! Tablets of 'Abdu'l-Bahá, Letters of Shoghi Effendi and Historical Notes about Japan. Japan: Bahá'í Publishing Trust, 1974.

Jeffery, Arthur. *The Foreign Vocabulary of the Qur'án.* Gaekward Oriental Series. Baroda: 1938.

Maḥmúd's Diary. See Zarqání, *Kitáb-i-Badáyi'u'l-Át͟hár.*

al-Munjid fi'l-A'lám. (Middle East Encyclopaedia). Beirut: Dáru'l-Mas͟hriq, 1969.

Nabíl-i-A'ẓam (Muḥammad-i-Zarandí). *The Dawn-Breakers.* Nabíl's Narrative of the Early Days of the Bahá'í Revelation. Wilmette, Illinois: Bahá'í Publishing Trust, 1932. London: Bahá'í Publishing Trust, 1953.

Ruhe, David S. *Door of Hope.* A Century of the Bahá'í Faith in the Holy Land. Oxford: George Ronald, 1983.

Shoghi Effendi. *The Advent of Divine Justice.* Wilmette, Illinois: Bahá'í Publishing Trust, rev. edn 1969.

—— *God Passes By.* Wilmette, Illinois: Bahá'í Publishing Trust, 7th repr. 1974.

—— *Messages to the Bahá'í World, 1950–1957.* Wilmette, Illinois: Bahá'í Publishing Trust, repr. 1971.

—— *The Promised Day Is Come.* Wilmette, Illinois: Bahá'í Publishing Trust, rev. edn 1980.

—— *The World Order of Bahá'u'lláh.* Wilmette, Illinois: Bahá'í Publishing Trust, 2nd rev. edn 1974.

Synopsis and Codification of the Laws and Ordinances of the Kitáb-i-Aqdas. Haifa: Bahá'í World Centre, 1973.

World Order. New York: World Order, vol. 4, April, 1938 to March, 1939.

Zarqání, Mírzá Maḥmúd-i-. *Kitáb-i-Badáyi'u'l-Át͟hár.* Bombay: vol. 1, 1914; vol. 2, 1921.